SOUTHERN

WRITERS

in the

MODERN WORLD

SOUTHERN

WRITERS

in the

MODERN

WORLD

DONALD DAVIDSON

EUGENIA DOROTHY BLOUNT LAMAR

MEMORIAL LECTURES, 1957

Delivered at Mercer University on November 20 and 21

This book is provided by a grant
from the
National Endowment for the Humanities

UNIVERSITY OF GEORGIA PRESS

ATHENS

Contents

Foreword

THESE LECTURES, DELIVERED AT MERCER UNIVERSITY IN NO-
vember 1957, inaugurated the Eugenia Dorothy Blount
Lamar Memorial Lectureship. This lectureship was made
possible by a bequest to Mercer University from the late
Mrs. Lamar, who stipulated that income from the legacy
should be used "to provide lectures of the very highest
type of scholarship which will aid in the permanent preservation of the values of Southern culture, history, and
literature."

Throughout her long and interesting life from birth in
1867 to death in 1955, Eugenia Dorothy Blount Lamar
was identified with the best in the Southern tradition. A
native of Jones County, Georgia, she spent most of her
life in Macon, where she was a leader in cultural, religious,
political, and social affairs for nearly three quarters of a
century. Happily married to Walter Douglas Lamar, this
Southern gentlewoman made her hearthstone a center of
hospitality and gracious living.

And yet "Miss Dolly," as Mrs. Lamar was widely and
affectionately known, exerted an influence far beyond the
home. From the example of her distinguished father, Con-
gressman James Henderson Blount, she was inspired to

regard public service as her first concern. Of the Southern gentry by breeding and inheritance, she was also a member in her own right of the natural aristocracy of virtue and talent. To her the public welfare and *noblesse oblige* were inseparably linked. The preservation of the past for the instruction and inspiration of posterity was with her a sacred trust. Tirelessly she worked until Sidney Lanier, the native poet of her beloved Macon, was accorded a rightful place in the Hall of Fame. To commemorate the valor of the Confederacy was her constant concern as Historian-General and President-General of the United Daughters of the Confederacy and as Georgia director of the foundation to preserve Stratford, the birthplace of Robert E. Lee. In the cultural life of Macon her generosity, as well as that of her husband, is represented in the Macon Little Theatre Building. But always first in her affection and philanthropy was the First Presbyterian Church, the church of her fathers.

From the days of her childhood when she looked across Tattnall Square toward the spires of Mercer University, that institution had a place in her heart. This cherished bond was duly recognized in 1940, for it was then she proudly received the honorary degree Doctor of Laws from the University. It is to the memory of this alumna, a great lady of the South, that Mercer University dedicates these lectures with admiration and respect.

Mrs. Lamar would have approved heartily the selection of Donald Davidson, a leading critic and poet of the Southern Literary Renascence, as the inaugural Lamar Lecturer, for he, as she, represents neither the Old nor the New but the Everlasting South.

MALCOLM LESTER, *Chairman*
The Lamar Lecture Committee

Mercer University
Macon, Georgia

Preface

THE INVITATION TO GIVE THE LECTURES PUBLISHED IN THIS
book came to me in early July, 1957, not long after I had
arrived in Vermont to teach, as in many summers previous,
at the Bread Loaf School of English of Middlebury College. To be asked by Mercer University to appear as inaugural lecturer under the Lamar Fund was a great honor;
but the task before me was also great. The only stipulation
as to subject was that I deal in some fashion with Southern
literature — a subject decidedly not uppermost in my mind
at the moment. I asked leave of Dean Malcolm Lester to
postpone choice of a subject, and he very kindly in-
dulged me.

Just about that time my summer neighbor, Robert Frost,
came up the road to give his usual intimate poetry reading
and talk for the Bread Loaf School. In his preliminary remarks Frost kept emphasizing in his sidelong, riddling way
the merits of "insubordination" as an American trait. He
made no political references, yet "insubordination" kept
running along as an undertone in his reading and comment. It was impossible not to connect it with the hot
debate then developing in Congress on "Civil Rights."
When I spoke to Frost after his reading, he said, banter-
ingly: "You've been 'insubordinate' down there!" My

guarded reply was, "I can't imagine what you mean." But Frost knew and I knew that I could and did imagine. He added a question that I could not answer at the time: "Do you suppose they'll send troops into the South?"

There was no connection that I can identify between Frost's remarks on that July evening and my ultimate choice of a subject for these lectures. Yet, as the summer wore on, my mind did keep turning more and more to my companions of the nineteen-twenties and the years just previous and after. Ransom, Tate, Warren, Moore, and others rose to my inner vision — young, vehement, resolute. As "Fugitives" and then as "Agrarians" we had indeed carried through an experiment in "insubordination" entirely outside the political realm and far-reaching in many of its implications. It was not for me to pass upon the merits of the experiment, but I could recall its commanding vibration — or could at least describe its true nature and aims in a somewhat reminiscent vein, with whatever critical perspective I could muster. That was, really, the only approach to the general subject of Southern literature that my immediate circumstances encouraged; perhaps it was the only approach I was qualified to use.

I finished and indeed largely composed the lectures in the midst of the turbulent and anxious scenes that accompanied the opening of Southern schools in the autumn of 1957 — grateful for the relief of mind that the act of reminiscence afforded. And no less grateful was I later to find myself in Macon, among familiar Georgia scenes, in company with gracious friends old and new, who needed no preparation to share recollection with me and undoubtedly supplemented my rememberings with their own. To them, to Mercer University, to Georgia, I owe very special thanks.

The lectures do not in any sense propose to be a definitive "history" of the movements discussed. As "history" they are incomplete. They embody the recollections and interpretations of only one participant. For publication I have filled in the text of the first two lectures, as given orally, with some slight additions of material omitted during the occasion for lack of time. The third lecture is reconstructed from notes but represents substantially what was said.

Returning to Robert Frost, I should add that he belongs in this account for a particular reason. It was Frost who, as "reader," recommended for publication John Crowe Ransom's first book, *Poems About God.*

DONALD DAVIDSON

Vanderbilt University
Nashville, Tennessee

LECTURE

ONE

The Thankless Muse and Her Fugitive Poets

IN THE NINETEEN-TWENTIES THE LAST THING EXPECTED OF A really ambitious young Southerner was that he would devote himself for some years, or even so much as a year or month, to the art of poetry alone — seriously, high-heartedly, exclusively, as if nothing else mattered but to write poetry and explore its every aspect. That not one young Southerner but a closely joined group, more or less fortuitously assembled at Nashville, should indulge themselves to this extent, from about 1920 to 1927, was a ridiculous aberration that the Merchants and Manufacturers Associations and the Booster Clubs of various cities might have deplored if it had not seemed so utterly, so absurdly unimportant. There was no commercial profit in poetry, but there was nothing dangerous either. Poetry did not affect the price of cotton or the value of real estate in Atlanta or Miami. It did not raise any questions among the clerics as to the Virgin Birth; or among scientists as to their secular sanctification of the theory of evolution. Seemingly, poetry offered no threat to the multiplication of textile mills or the industrial growth of Birmingham. It could

1

neither hurt nor help the Democratic Party, which was licking its wounds and trying to get patched up after its disastrous international adventure under Woodrow Wilson. Perhaps poetry did have a little something to do with education, but neither Chancellor Kirkland of Vanderbilt nor any other college president of the nineteen-twenties could have suspected that the obscure poetic activities of certain young instructors and their students would ever be either an asset or a liability to an institution of higher learning.

So the young Southerners who from 1922 to 1925 published *The Fugitive,* a magazine devoted entirely to poetry (most of it their own), and who later came to be known as the Fugitive group — these rash adventurers could be ignored and as a matter of course were largely ignored by the South that was using as its mirror of wellbeing the front page of the newspaper, or the society page, or the stock market quotations. And that was, really, a very happy situation for John Crowe Ransom, Allen Tate, Robert Penn Warren, Merrill Moore, Walter Clyde Curry, Sidney Hirsch, and others of the group, including myself.[1] The greatest of all privileges, in a sense, is the privilege of being let alone — of being neither promoted, nor subsidized, nor regulated, nor suppressed, nor interfered with in any way. Perhaps this is one of the great unchartered American rights and underlies those that are specifically chartered in the United States Constitution. Whether privilege or right, it is something that the South of tradition has always understood very well and has warmly defended. The Fugitives enjoyed the privilege in full measure.

1. In 1921 there were seven members of the group: Donald Davidson, James Marshall Frank, Sidney Mttron-Hirsch, Stanley Johnson, John Crowe Ransom, Alec B. Stevenson, and Allen Tate. Soon Walter Clyde Curry, Merrill Moore, William Yandell Elliott, and William Frierson joined. Later Jesse Wills, Ridley Wills, Robert Penn Warren, Laura Riding (Gottschalk), and Alfred Starr appeared on the Fugitive roster.

They could of course have asked themselves the questions that one of our rather distant cousins asked himself three centuries ago when the fellowship he sought went to a more up-and-coming man, and he found himself at Horton, with time on his hands, and nothing to do but compose poetry:

> Alas! What boots it with uncessant care
> To tend the homely slighted shepherd's trade,
> And strictly meditate the thankless Muse?
> Were it not better done as others use,
> To sport with *Amaryllis* in the shade,
> Or with the tangles of *Neaera's* hair?

But we did not for the time being debate or even consider Cousin John Milton's somewhat rhetorical questions. We did not need to ask whether the Muse were thankless, so long as we found excitement, week by week, year by year in strictly meditating, as indeed we did, the art of poetry. We meditated almost nothing else besides. The Vanderbilt campus of those days, with its few brick buildings scattered among fine trees and good Middle Tennessee bluegrass, was our Horton; and since Vanderbilt then, actually was — as it is not now — on the western border of a Southern city not very much expanded, the residential area of West End surrounding the campus was but a step from a rural countryside. I do not know, and I do not think the scholars know, what alternative choices in poetry, or I might say temptations, Cousin John Milton was referring to in his cryptic lines about sporting with Amaryllis and Neaera. But if Edna St. Vincent Millay could be taken as a sort of Amaryllis and Gertrude Stein as a Neaera in the nineteen-twenties, I can say without hesitation that they did not tempt us in the slightest. Nor were we inclined to ask ourselves whether the price of cotton, the value of real estate, the industrialization of the South, the state of religion, or the state of science was either profitable or dangerous for the state of poetry. We were concerned with strictly meditating the Muse, thankless or not. The meditation was very strict, but paradoxically it was also enthusiastic.

Strict and enthusiastic are the right adjectives, I believe, and discipline and excitement would be the right nouns, to characterize an experience that for some years was an extraordinary mingling of the formal and informal. This is the experience that I want to describe, first of all as something possessing and possessed by these young poets as poets — and therefore no doubt common to poets in all ages and places; and, second, as an experience that maybe was peculiarly Southern in that no such thing had happened before in American literary history, and possibly could never have happened but at this particular place at this particular time.

There have been coteries of poets before, of course, who gathered regularly and read their verses to one another. For example, the Rhymers' Club, which William Butler Yeats helped to found in London, partly out of loneliness and desire for literary company. But the gatherings of the Rhymers' Club — to judge from Yeats' own account — must have been a compound of Bohemianism, speechifying, and *fin de siècle* melancholy — with Irish nationalism there too, jostling Pater-worship a little impolitely, while Lionel Johnson and Yeats took turns at monologuing. A Fugitive meeting was nothing like that. Nor could it have resembled any gathering of the Latter Day Saints of New England, whether at Concord or Brook Farm or the Saturday Club. And I can certify that a Fugitive meeting could not possibly have resembled a meeting of any of the poetry societies that sprang up during the rise of the New Poetry — not even of that gallant and, I think, most remarkable of all the poetry societies of the nineteen-twenties, the Poetry Society of South Carolina, which held — and still holds — its meetings in historic South Carolina Hall at Charleston and which then listed on its roster of members, either as practicing poets or patrons, the great names of Charleston and South Carolina: I mean the Heywards, Hugers, Manigaults, Middletons, Pinckneys, Ravenels, Stoneys, Warings, and such others. This particular aspect of the *noblesse oblige* principle was not so well preserved at Nashville, although we did receive certain donations that, added to magazine subscriptions, enabled us to meet the modest expenses of publication and to offer poetry prizes.[2]

Yet we were somehow within the general Southern tradition in having attachments that could be taken as a matter of course. We were not detached — not completely detached — for we could assume that we belonged in an existing, rather stable society as persons if not as poets. I say this despite the rather too impudent Foreword affixed to the first issue of *The Fugitive,* in which we lightly announced that "The Fugitive flees from nothing faster than from the high caste Brahmins of the Old South."[3] This

2. In various issues of *The Fugitive* acknowledgments were made to the following as either "patrons" or as donors of prizes: Esther Antheil, Ithaca, N. Y.; The Associated Retailers of Nashville; Joel Cheek, Nashville; William C. Cobb, Nashville; Mrs. H. S. Coil, Cincinnati, Ohio; Curtis T. Everett, Bombay, India; Simon Ghertner, Nashville; Mrs. Isabel R. Mayers, Los Angeles; Mrs. Kenneth McColl, Bennettsville, Ga.; Prof. C. A. McMurray, Nashville; Mr. and Mrs. F. A. Sherrer, Oberlin, O.; Mrs. Evelyn Stevenson, Nashville; Ward-Belmont College, Nashville; several anonymous donors.

3. The complete text of the passage (*The Fugitive,* Vol. I, No. 1, April, 1922) is as follows:

"Official exception having been taken by the sovereign people to the mint julep, a literary phase known rather euphemistically as Southern literature has expired, like any other stream whose source is stopped up. The demise was not untimely; among other advantages, *The Fugitive* is enabled to come to birth in Nashville, Tennessee, under a star not entirely unsympathetic. *The Fugitive* flees from nothing faster than from the high caste Brahmins of the Old South. Without raising the question of whether the blood in the veins of its editors runs red, they at any rate are not advertising it as blue; indeed, as to pedigree, they cheerfully invite the most unfavorable inference from the circumstances of their anonymity."

meant simply that we wanted our poetry to be judged on its merits. We asked no indulgence for our verses on the ground that we were Southerners — as some of the lady poet laureates of the South at the time seemed to be doing.

But as to attachments and assumptions, it is only the backward look that now allows me to distinguish them as a kind of discovery. Our great good fortune was that we shared pretty much the same assumptions about society, about man, nature, and God. And we were most fortunate in not even having to ask ourselves whether or not we were on common ground in such matters. As yet we did not know that we were lucky in being able to assume that we had common assumptions. We did much thinking, but there were some important matters that we did not have to think about. It was a blessed sort of ignorance, and I believe it marked us as definitely Southern. It was, in fact, a condition of being Southern-born. In the South of those days there was a great deal that could be taken for granted. There were many questions that did not need to be asked, and some of these were large metaphysical questions.

Later on when Allen Tate, like the rest of us, found that the metaphysical questions would, after all, have to be argued, he dramatized our former state of innocence (or was it maturity?) in his poem, "To the Lacedaemonians," in which an old Confederate veteran is represented as speaking to his imaginary comrades:

> I was a boy, I never knew cessation
> Of the bright course of blood along the vein;
> Moved, an old dog by me, to field and stream
> In the speaking ease of the fall rain;
> When I was a boy, the light upon the hills
> Was there because I could see it, not because
> Some special gift of God had put it there.[4]

And in Tate's "Causerie," I find this passage:

4. *Poems, 1922-1947*, p. 15.

> What is this conversation, now secular,
> A speech not mine yet speaking for me in
> The heaving jelly of my tribal air?
> It rises in the throat, it climbs the tongue,
> It perches there for secret tutelage
> And gets it, of inscrutable instruction —
> Which is a puzzle, like crepuscular light
> That has no visible source . . . .[5]

One of our attachments was to an institution. Vanderbilt University, though boastful about its modernity, was then like an Oxford college in its relaxed and casual indifference to what young men like us might be doing with our time. The other attachment was to the city, Nashville, superficially one of the least inviting of Southern cities; yet in its jumble of old and new tendencies that both attracted and revolted, it somehow bound us to it.

I do not know which one of these attachments was the more important. I do know that it was possible then for a young Southern poet to pass from university to city, from city to university, without any great sense of shock. Both were describable as "home." Both were, indistinguishably, provinces of an *alma mater* that might be found at one hour in a class-room where Dean Herbert Cushing Tolman was expounding Sophocles' ὕβρις φυτεύει τύραννον; or where John Crowe Ransom was analyzing the controlled irregularities of meter in a poem by Thomas Hardy; and at some other hour, very likely near midnight, in the pleasant James Frank home far out on Whitland Avenue, where Allen Tate might be arguing that the form did indeed "require the myth" in his newly composed "Horatian Epode to the Duchess of Malfi," and that the form was, furthermore, a true epode, not just a loose assemblage of verses as some of the Fugitives present, stiffly clutching their typed carbons of his poem, stoutly averred it to be.

5. *Ibid.,* p. 81.

Perhaps I interpret the group experience too much in terms of my own experience. Yet memory tells me that for us in these first years the pursuit of poetry as an art was the conclusion of the whole matter of living, learning, and being. It subsumed everything, but it was also as natural and reasonable an act as conversation on the front porch. We dropped into the cousinship of poetry as unhesitatingly as—in those times of unabridged hospitality—one dropped into the house of kinsman or friend, without invitation or prearrangement. It was as if we had been cousins all the time, or had had good report of one another through some aunt, uncle, or grandparent.

This metaphor, like other metaphors of Fugitive poetry, does not propose to explain anything. It states or represents something that cannot be explained in terms of fact. I do not think the literary historian can ever explain, by piecing together bits of fact and theorizing from cause to effect, just how this particular group of young men happened to become a group of poets in Nashville, Tennessee. But any Southerner that has not lost his grip on the continuity of his tradition can imagine through the metaphor what our cousinship was like. Yet the metaphor must have some correspondence with solid reality and not be merely fantastic. Else what becomes of "the world's body"? That phrase is John Ransom's. He came to it later on in another outreaching of metaphor. But always he was, as he politely declared at many a Fugitive meeting, "literal-minded" — a term he used just before rending to bits with calm, analytical pincers some too airy fancy that one of us had bounced into in a mere fit of rhyme.

I will give some of the solid reality, or world's body, of the metaphor. I do it in about the same terms your mother or a beloved aunt would use if you asked her just why those six or eight people out of all the people in the country happened to drop in unexpectedly and get invited to dinner.

Like all such Southern accounts, my account begins with kinfolks and place associations. It was this way. My Uncle Wallace Wells — who was my mother's youngest brother and was just ten years older than I — was a senior in Branham and Hughes Preparatory School when I entered as a freshman. On graduation, my uncle entered Vanderbilt University — and, incidentally, played center on one of Dan McGugin's football teams. So, when I graduated, I naturally entered Vanderbilt University — in 1909, on a $100 loan and a little odd cash. That was not enough money, though it was eked out by further loans and more odd cash. I barely held out through the freshman year at Vanderbilt, then dropped out to teach school for four years. When I returned in the autumn of 1914, I found myself studying Shakespeare under John Crowe Ransom.

John Ransom had graduated in 1909 from Vanderbilt and had finished at Oxford as a Rhodes Scholar. The latter distinction, in those years, gave singular eminence. But John Ransom was born at Pulaski, Tennessee, just a few miles from where I was born, and my father, who was a teacher, knew John Ransom's father, who was a Methodist preacher. Ransom's sister, Ellene, was in classes with me at Vanderbilt, and I soon came to know the whole Ransom family.

Among my Vanderbilt classmates were Alec B. Stevenson, William Yandell Elliott, and Stanley Johnson, all of whom studied under Ransom and under Walter Clyde Curry of South Carolina, then a young instructor, and Dr. Edwin Mims, an Arkansas man, lately come from Trinity College, North Carolina, to be the new head of the Vanderbilt English department. Alec Stevenson's father was a professor in the Vanderbilt School of Religion. William Elliott and Stanley Johnson belonged natively to Nashville and Middle Tennessee.

The two young instructors, Ransom and Curry, took a

good deal of genial personal interest in Stevenson, Elliott, Johnson, and myself. We were in fact not many years their juniors. A literary association grew up that antedated by some years the origin of the Fugitive group proper. Perhaps it was at first more of an intellectual association than a literary association, for what we undergraduates did of writing in those years was juvenile and collegiate. Only Ransom, at that time, was beginning to write; and after a while began fitfully to publish poetry that was serious and mature. It was the intellectual association that counted most, and the extra-curricular part counted as heavily as the curricular, if not more so. It would never have occurred to any of us that the higher learning could be obtained *only* through the instruction of a specialist in a regularly accredited course. Under Dr. Edwin Mims, to be sure, the English department had suddenly become a lively competitor with the classical studies that had been the staple of our formal education. For me there was excitement in Dr. Mims' courses, partly from the stunning revelation that English and American literature offered subjects to study, not just books to read. Long before coming to Vanderbilt, I had read all of Cooper, Scott, Poe, and other worthies that I could lay hands on, and my father was always quoting his long favorite passages from "The Vision of Sir Launfal" or the famous first sentence of Johnson's *Rasselas*. But somehow I had never dreamed that one studied Poe, or Lowell, or Johnson *at college!* When I reported this great discovery to my father, he only smiled indulgently, and said nothing.

But it was my friend Alec Stevenson who first led me to Joseph Conrad's novels, not any professor of modern fiction. It was red-headed Curtis T. Everett of Kentucky, another student friend, who introduced me to Dostoievski; and much earlier, in 1909 and 1910, it was Ben and Varnell Tate, the older brothers of Allen Tate, who gave me

the free run of the personal library that they had installed
in sectional bookcases in their room in Kissam Hall. With
special vividness I recall their de luxe edition of the complete works of Guy'de Maupassant — in translation. I read
that set through, volume by volume. Walter Clyde Curry
was my instructor in Chaucer, but from him I got, on the
side, out of his own library, an informal reading course in
modern European drama — Ibsen, Strindberg, Rostand,
Hauptmann, Sudermann, and the like.

In the city, however, was something very different, and
in the long run very important to us all. Through Stanley
Johnson I came to know the Jewish mystic and writer,
Sidney Hirsch. At the Hirsch apartment on Twentieth
Avenue, two blocks from the campus, we somehow began
to gather, afternoons and evenings, for long discussions.
These ranged through poetry to philosophy, but became
predominantly philosophical whenever in those years Ransom, Elliott, and Johnson led the conversation into some
logical dispute, as it seemed to me they too often did. Like
Stephen Dedalus in Joyce's *Portrait of the Artist* I felt
myself destined to be but a shy guest at the feast of the
world's great culture if the banquet were to consist of the
categories of Kant and the heresies of Hegel. I was not
much past twenty-one, and in philosophy had not pro-
gressed beyond a brain-battering semester's acquaintance
with Jevons' textbook of logic. I could reel off the medieval Latin of the mnemonic rhyme and perhaps could
identify a simple *barbara* syllogism if compelled to it, for
Dr. Herbert Sanborn, our professor of philosophy, was
stern about all that.

One could but be awed and obedient when Dr. Sanborn
strode vigorously to his desk, cloaked in all the Olympian
majesty of Leipzig and Heidelberg, and, without a book
or note before him, delivered a perfectly ordered lecture,
freely sprinkled with quotations from the original San-

skrit, Greek, Latin, German, French, or Italian, which of course he would not insult us by translating. Yet still I did not have the least idea about schools of philosophy or such philosophical terms as epistemology or ontology, and I knew nothing of Plato's theories, even though, like others, I had wrestled my way through the Apology and parts of the Crito and Phaedo in the original Greek, as was required of any prospective B.A. So I was but a listener when these discussions were under way. About the only memory of them I retain is of how stubbornly and constantly my friend Stanley Johnson engaged Ransom and Elliott in metaphysical combat, and how sternly he refused to give ground.

But they in turn fell silent and became listeners when — as always happened — Sidney Hirsch picked out some word — most likely a proper name like Odysseus or Hamlet or Parsifal, or some common word like *fool* or *fugitive* — and then, turning from dictionary to dictionary in various languages, proceeded to unroll a chain of veiled meanings that could be understood only through the system of etymologies to which he had the key. This, he assured us, was the wisdom of the ages — a palimpsest underlying all great poetry, all great art, all religion, in all eras, in all lands. All true poets possessed this wisdom intuitively, he told us, solemnly, repeatedly. Furthermore he proved it later on, when we began to forsake philosophy for poetry by pointing out that some image that had crept into our verses, no matter what we intended it to mean, revealed exactly the kind of mystic symbolism he had traced from the Ramayana to Homer to Sophocles to Dante to Shakespeare to William Blake. Probably no group of poets ever before received just this kind of assurance.

Reluctant we might be to accept Sidney Hirsch's etymologies, which took liberties with Grimm's law and walked over philology on high stilts. But his constant probing into mythologies and religions brought results that astounded some of us, even when we argued against him. Most of all, his declaration of the high eminence of poetry somehow elevated into an almost priestly rite the consideration of the most juvenile and humble of our verses. How had he won this curious secret knowledge? We did not know. He never told us. Disdaining formal schooling, he had roamed the world, it was said. In France he had frequented the studio of Rodin. He knew actors, singers, artists. His one-act play, "The Passion Play of Washington Square," was on one of the vaudeville circuits. I remember seeing it in Nashville. For Nashville he had composed a Greek pageant in verse, *The Fire Regained*. Miraculously, he had enlisted the combined artistic and educational resources of Nashville to stage it, in the open air, in front of the replica of the Parthenon. He was a Rosicrucian, he was a Cabbalist? He was? — we knew not what. But that did not seem to matter in 1914 or 1915 or 1916 when we could sit on the Hirsch balcony overlooking the campus and the roofs of West End — and endlessly converse.

Through Stanley Johnson, too, and Sidney Hirsch's sister Goldie Hirsch, I came into the company of other Nashvillians, especially a group of Southernized Jews and art-minded Gentiles that Stanley frequented. There were informal musical evenings when one found in some friendly house a little orchestra of flute, violins, and piano. There were visits to the Deutscher Verein, then flourishing, that brought together faculty members and students of both Vanderbilt University and Peabody College. Or there might be a private musical session in William Elliott's home with Bill soloing in bass while I ventured a fumbling accompaniment at the piano. Or it might be a holiday expedition up the Cumberland River on Horace Beall's little steamboat, for a literary al fresco affair among the oak trees — with Carrie Rich, Goldie Hirsch, and Willa

Tatom (later Mrs. Stanley Johnson) sure to be in the party. Or there were nights at the Vendome Theatre — to see *The Merry Widow,* or something from Victor Herbert, or Kennedy's *The Servant in the House,* or Forbes Robertson in *Hamlet,* or even Geraldine Farrar in *Madame Butterfly* — and afterwards the long walk back to the Vanderbilt campus where Halley's Comet was blazing across the sky above Kissam Hall. It was not exactly Bohemian; nor was it anything like a Parisian salon; but it was not academic, either.

One day of days I remember well. My teacher, John Ransom, beckoned me aside and led me to a shady spot on the campus near the streetcar stop called "Vanderbilt Stile" — though the stile had long since yielded to an open entrance. Ransom drew a sheet of paper from his pocket. Almost blushingly, he announced that he had written a poem. It was his very first, he said. He wanted to read it to me. He read it, and I listened — admiringly, you may be sure. The title of the poem was "Sunset." But in that moment, I suppose, was the actual dawn of the "Fugitive movement."

When the United States entered the war against Germany, we were all scattered. But for a while in the summer of 1917 Ransom and I were candidates for a reserve commission at the First Officers Training Camp, Fort Oglethorpe, Georgia. Now in campaign hats and khaki, we sat in a grove of pines on the battlefield of Chickamauga, at the foot of Snodgrass Hill. Again Ransom drew a manuscript from his pocket. This time it was a large sheaf of poems. Under the pines he read me parts of what was published in 1919 as *Poems About God,* by Lieutenant John Crowe Ransom. I carried with me to France, and back again, typed copies of some of the poems Ransom had read to me — still admiring, but puzzled, wondering much. I could write nothing of that kind. The meaning

of Ransom's poems came to me dim and distorted like
shapes glimpsed at the bottom of a Tennessee creek —
clear yet wavering, most incalculably shaken just at the
point of perception. When I read those poems in France,
by candlelight in some peasant's house in the Côte d'Or
or Yonne, or some ruined village near the Western Front,
they still blurred my exploring, eager eyes, even though
at that distance I could more gratefully recognize in them
the Tennessee country I had left. I was not only a long
way off from writing poetry. I did not even know how to
read poetry — if this was poetry, and surely it must be.

Then suddenly in 1920, as if the Muse herself had ar-
ranged our lives, we were all back at Vanderbilt again,
teachers and students once more, the same group, with
notable additions. The very first of these was Allen Tate
in whom, much as if we had met "Cousin Poe" on some
campus walk, we instantly knew the poet.[6] Of course Dr.
Edwin Mims assisted the Muse by giving Stanley Johnson
and myself appointments as instructors while we pursued
graduate studies in English. A little to my surprise, I found
that Ransom was discontented with the poems I had carried around in manuscript and now could read in print.
He had taken a new turn and was writing sonnets — mostly
in the Shakespearean form. In fact he and Curry had been
engaged in a kind of sonnet *flyting* — firing strings of sonnets back and forth at one another in typescript. Ransom
was apparently in the lead with what almost amounted to
a sonnet sequence. Later, I believe, Ransom, still discontented, destroyed these numerous sonnets. I saw no more
of them after a while, except the one or two that appear,
remodelled, in his *Chills and Fever*.

The newcomers drawn into our cousinship of poetry
were not, in a Southern sense, exactly strangers. Allen

6. Cf. "Our Cousin, Mr. Poe," in Tate's *The Forlorn Demon*.

Tate was, after all, the young brother of Ben and Varnell
Tate, whom I had known in 1909-10. I first knew Robert
Penn Warren when he turned up in an English class I was
teaching — a freckled, angular, gawky boy, yet a prodigy
whom at birth the Muse had apparently vested with a complete literary equipment. Warren's home was Guthrie,
Kentucky, across the Tennessee line near the "black to-
bacco" country of Robertson County, where I had first
taught school and heard the story of the Bell Witch. Mer-
rill Moore was the son of John Trotwood Moore, the
Tennessee writer, whom we all knew — as we also knew
Merrill's mother, his grandmother, and his twin sisters
Mary Daniel and Helen. Jesse Wills was the cousin of
Ridley Wills, whom I had known as a fraternity brother;
it was a West Tennessee family. Tate, Warren, Moore, and
Wills were all Vanderbilt undergraduates.

Here my long-drawn-out metaphor reaches its period at
last. Eligibility for membership in the group — as yet un-
named — did not of course depend upon family connection, place of birth, fraternity affiliation, or registration in
Vanderbilt. The only qualification was ability to write
poetry. Campus acquaintance, in or out of class, made it
easy to discover that ability. But the question might be
asked: Why did a Fugitive group arise on the Vanderbilt
campus in Nashville, Tennessee, and nowhere else? The
answer must be speculative. The fact is that no similar
group appeared anywhere in the North or West, even
though at this time the poetry we call "modern" was reach-
ing the height of its prestige and all the leading American
figures — Frost, Robinson, Millay, Sandburg, Amy Lowell
— were Northerners or Midwesterners. I will venture an
hypothesis on which an answer might be based. Suppose
that Ransom had been a Californian, Tate a native of
Iowa, Warren of Kansas, Davidson of Maine, Hirsch of
New York, and so on; and suppose that we had somehow

assembled at Nashville, through scholarship aid or the magnetic attraction of Dan McGugin's football teams. Would this Fugitive group then have appeared, even if we had had exactly the same degree of literary interest and ability? I cannot imagine such a phenomenon. There would have been individual poets, no doubt, and they might have known each other, even casually worked together, but there would not have been a "group" in any cohesive sense, much less this particular "Fugitive group."

Then if you ask me why, of all places, at Nashville, and why not at Charleston, Charlottesville, Atlanta, Macon, Athens, New Orleans, I can say only that I can see no good reason why not if, granting ability and interest, the poets of such Southern centers had applied themselves to the art of poetry as exclusively as we did for a long while at Nashville. That the other Southern poets of this period did not practice this serious, exclusive devotion to their art seems clear from the record. Either they were caught up in the superficial excitement that attended the "New Poetry" and practiced facile imitation of its merely rhetorical features without asking themselves any very hard critical questions or submitting to the discipline of high art; or else they were in equally uncritical revolt against modernism and were imitating the rhetoric of nineteenth century poetry without any question as to its artistic premises. Thus, whether rebels or reactionaries, they slid into a false kind of self-consciousness that put them into a wrong relation both to their present and their past, and so lost the inherited advantages that, as Southern poets, they should have enjoyed. They also were unable to utilize effectively for the purposes of high art the advantages offered them through the various poetry societies and little magazines that were striving to provide an audience for poetry.

By the autumn of 1921 our group was meeting regularly,

once more with Sidney Hirsch, but since Sidney — whom we now began to call Dr. Hirsch — was living with his brother-in-law, James M. Frank, our assembly-place was the Frank home on Whitland Avenue. That meant a street-car ride, before and after meetings; we were still years away from automobile ownership. Generally we met once a week, on Saturday evenings. There was no formal organization. Each brought to the meeting whatever new poems he had composed during the days preceding, always providing typed copies for the circle. Each in turn read his poem or poems. Then all took part in a relentless critical discussion. Within less than a year there was a good-sized accumulation of manuscripts, and we readily agreed with Hirsch's suggestion that we publish a magazine of poetry. It seemed highly appropriate to adopt Alec Stevenson's proposal that we name the magazine *The Fugitive*.[7] The name was to us by that time a familiar symbol, expounded to us in its many transformations by Sidney Hirsch, and it had other attractive features. We did not realize how difficult it would be, later on, to explain the choice of name, or what satirical interpretations it might invite. At first we selected poems for publication by ballot of the group, and avoided designation of an editor. The first number came forth in April, 1922. In that issue and the following June issue we appeared under pen-names.

I do not propose to go into the history of the magazine itself. I am here concerned with what principally emerged from our experience of strictly meditating the Muse — that is, rather steadily composing poems to be read in our close-knit group — composing them in a spirit of friendly emulation, week by week, often in great and joyous excitement, but sometimes, too, with more determination than fervor; then submitting the new creations to run the gant-

7. This is according to my personal recollection. We kept no "Minutes."

let of criticism and argument, inside the Fugitive meeting itself or in more intimate and personal colloquies between individuals.

Looking back from a distance of thirty-five years I can see how tentative and experimental much of our poetry was in those Fugitive days. All of us except Ransom were veritable apprentices to the art. From the very first number to the last, much of Ransom's best poetry appeared in *The Fugitive.* The same could not be said for some of the rest of us. We were young men, striking out a little wildly. Ransom was five years older than I, and eleven years older than Tate. His performance was authoritative, and so was his criticism. It was natural that some of the prominent public notices we received should single out Ransom, the already mature and published writer, as the leader of a coterie in which the rest seemed in greater or less degree satellites. It would be more correct to say that Ransom, the most advanced, was the first to choose his orbit; then others, one by one, found theirs, exerting great mutual attraction, with perhaps some repulsion here and there, upon one another. An early poem of Ransom's bears upon this general matter. It appeared as the first poem in the first issue of *The Fugitive:*

EGO[8]
By John Crowe Ransom

You have heard something muttered in my scorn:
"A little learning addleth this man's wit,
He crieth on our dogmas Counterfeit!
And no man's bubble 'scapeth his sharp thorn;

"Nor he respecteth duly our tall steeple,
But in his pride turning from book to book

8. The title and text are as first published in *The Fugitive.* In 1924 Ransom included the poem in his *Chills and Fever* under the new title, "Plea in Mitigation." He omitted the next to the last stanza and made other small changes.

Heareth our noise and hardly offereth look,
Nor liveth neighborly with these the people."

With reason, friends, I am complained upon,
Who am a headstrong man, sentenced from birth
To love unusual gods beyond all earth
And the easy gospels bruited hither and yon.

So I bring hurt upon my own sweet kin,
And on my scholars, the young simple snails,
Treading their tumuli to holy grails:
I make reproach, and then these griefs begin.

For no man loves to seem so small of grace,
And I could wish me too born dull, born blind,
If I might not estrange my gentle kind,
Nor brag, nor run a solitary race.

Friends, come acquit me of that stain of pride:
Much has been spoken solemnly together,
And you have heard my heart; so answer whether
I am so proud a Fool, and godless beside.

Sages and friends, too often have you seen us
Deep in the midnight conclave as we used;
For my part, reverently were you perused;
No rank or primacy being hatched between us;

For my part, much beholden to you all,
Giving a little and receiving more;
Learning had stuffed this head with but lean lore
Betwixt the front bone and the occipital;

Anatomy, that doled these dubious features,
Had housed within me, close to my breastbone,
My Demon, always clamoring Up, Begone,
Pursue your gods faster than most of creatures;

So I take not the vomit where they do,
Comporting downwards to the general breed;
I have run further, matching your heat and speed,
And tracked the Wary Fugitive with you;

And if an alien miserably at feud
With those my generation, I have reason
To think to salve the fester of my treason;
A seven of friends exceeds much multitude.

There is no other poem that tells, as this one does, how close we were in affection and, as poets, how we felt ourselves suspect by the world because we were poets. But as to the paths, or orbits, that we followed, these were alike in some of their co-ordinates, however different in other respects. This is the way in which I would plot likenesses or agreements.

First, we gave strict attention, from the beginning, to the *form* of poetry. The very nature of our meetings facilitated and intensified such attention, and probably influenced Fugitive habits of composition. Every poem was read aloud by the poet himself, while the members of the group had before them typed copies of the poem. The reading aloud might be followed by a murmur of compliments, but often enough there was a period of ruminative silence before anyone said a word. Then discussion began, and it was likely to be ruthless in its exposure of any technical weakness as to rhyme, meter, imagery, metaphor and was often minute in analysis of details. Praise for good performance was rarely lacking, though some excellent poems might find the group sharply divided in judgment. But even the best poems might exhibit some imperfection in the first draft. It was understood that our examination would be skeptical. A poem had to prove its strength, if possible its perfection, in all its parts. The better the poem, the greater the need for a perfect finish. Any inequality in technical performance was sure to be detected. It was not enough for a poem to be impressive in a general way. Poems that were merely pleasant, or conventional, or mediocre did not attract much comment. But this regular procedure hardly ever could be strictly applied to the work of Merrill Moore, who was likely to appear at a meeting with anywhere from six to twenty poems, and if one was criticized, he rarely stopped to argue, but blithely and amiably went on to the next.

This process of intensive criticism, characteristic of the Fugitive meetings, carried over into private conversation between meetings when we could discuss our poems more informally. It was still more highly developed in the correspondence and exchange of manuscripts that went on when this or that member was absent from Nashville. I venture to say that this latter type of criticism was most beneficial, because it allowed deliberation. The most helpful criticism I ever received — and the sternest — was from Allen Tate, in the marginal notations on manuscripts that I sent him and in the very frank letters that always came with the return of a manuscript. Meanwhile, too, some of us were students in Ransom's advanced writing course, in which he developed a similar type of commentary, scrutinized selected poems of past and present, and went heavily into theories of prosody.

In its cumulative effect this severe discipline made us self-conscious craftsmen, abhorring looseness of expression, perfectly aware that a somewhat coldblooded process of revision, after the first ardor of creation had subsided, would do no harm to art. It also led to what we sometimes called a "packed" line. The poet, anxious to fortify his verses against criticism, strove to weed out anything "loose." This "tightening up" might produce a poetry far less fluent and easy than was the current fashion. But this tendency could become a vice, and perhaps in some instances it did.

I am not prepared to say whether or not, as Southerners, the Fugitives showed a preference for the traditional forms of poetry because they belonged to a society that, out of ancient habit, cherished the formal element in its fundamental relationships. At any rate we were early concerned with the problem of what concessions should be made to experimentalism in the arts. Would we, for example, admit "free verse" as a valid form? How far could rhyme and meter be dispensed with, or, if not dispensed with, distorted? What innovations of diction and meter could be allowed? What license as to language?

We seemed to hold that the great tradition of poetry from Homer on down clearly established the formal element as indispensable. The poet sacrificed it at his peril in favor of any relatively formless improvisation. But, like some other moderns — though not for the same reasons necessarily—we could not grant that Tennyson and Browning, or nineteenth century poetry in general, offered very sound examples of the application of the formal element of poetry. We turned back to Shakespeare and Milton, but not, in these early years, to Donne and the metaphysical poets. Among the moderns we preferred such adaptations of traditional form as could be found in Hardy and Yeats, with Tate insisting also on the great relevance of Baudelaire. Except for Tate, we were not as yet admirers of Eliot. Yet we were perfectly ready to concede some merit to modern experimentation — even to "free verse" — on two conditions: (1) the experiment must stand as severe a test as to form and technique as any other of the rhetorics of poetry; the mere novelty of experimentalism allowed no immunity from such criticism; (2) mastery of traditional forms was a prerequisite to valid experimentalism; to deviate from traditional forms without first practicing them was to ignore the total resources of the art and engage in irresponsible dilettantism.

In the October, 1922, issue of *The Fugitive* John Crowe Ransom wrote — partly by way of comment on Robert Graves' discussion of English poetry —

Many genuine talents receive a genuine inspiration and then dissipate the energies that ought to go into creation in a blind agony about the form. . . . it would seem at least likely that the determinate mathematical regularities of meter which are imposed upon the words have as much to do with the total effect of a poem as, in a sister art, the determinate geometrical regularities of outline which are imposed upon the stones have to do with the total effect of a work of architecture.

But one cannot dogmatize here. The charming personality of Graves expresses itself without embarrassment in prosodical verse. But some of the most brilliant of contemporary minds have apparently been unable to do this. To us even who have every encouragement to be traditionalists, their work at some points seems so perfected that we would not wish it to be otherwise, their phrases so final as not to admit the suggestion of change. In illustration we want nothing better to cite than the Horatian Epode of Allen Tate's which appears in these pages. We do not believe that these words could be altered without lowering the given plane of sophistication, and that would only be to destroy one beauty on the lean prospect of getting another one.

And I, too, would want nothing better to cite than this poem of Allen Tate's. It brought about a very hot and prolonged discussion in the Fugitive circle. It will still bear up under close inspection.

HORATIAN EPODE TO THE DUCHESS OF MALFI[9]
By Allen Tate

The stage is about to be swept of corpses.
You have no more chance than an infusorian
Lodged in a hollow molar of an eohippus.
Come, now, no prattle of remergence with the ὄντως ὄν.

As (the form requires the myth)
A Greek girl stood once in the prytaneum
Of Carneades, hearing mouthings of Probability,
Then mindful of love dashed her brain on a megalith

9. *The Fugitive,* Vol. I, No. 2 (October, 1922)

So you, O nameless Duchess who die young,
Meet death somewhat lovingly
And I am filled with a pity of beholding skulls.
There was no pride like yours.

Now considerations of the void coming after
Not changed by the "strict gesture" of your death
Split the straight line of pessimism
Into two infinities.

It is moot whether there be divinities
As I finish this play by Webster:
The street-cars are still running however,
And the catharsis fades in the warm water of a yawn.

The "Horatian Epode" may still arouse debate. But
here, certainly, in 1922, was no waste of creation in a
"blind agony about the form." Young Allen Tate (then
23 years old) knew his Horace in the Latin and his Pindar
in the Greek. He was already skilled in prosody. The intended irregularities of his "Horatian Epode" had old
precedent and new application. When he wrote the last
two lines —

The street-cars are still running, however,
And the catharsis fades in the warm water of a yawn.

he was, he could argue, no more impudent than Horace
had been in various odes or epodes. His experiment was
no accident; and though, like much other Fugitive verse
of this period, it could be taken as an exercise, it nevertheless had in it an underlying conviction about the nature
of reality.

But what is the nature of reality, and how does the
underlying conviction of the poet take hold of it if it is to
be expressed in the literary forms used by poets? Perhaps
our poems were often experiments or exercises, but even
an exercise in poetry insists on having a subject, and conviction about reality filters in if the poet is at all serious.
The only alternative is to have no conviction, and then

the poem proposes to be neutral and noncommittal, as is the way of "Pure Poetry." Pure Poetry is, presumably, a poetry that has no intellectual or moral content, like the Imagist poetry. It intends — in Archibald MacLeish's phrase — not to "mean" but to "be." By and large we rejected this false antithesis. The poem must both "mean" and "be." Of our membership, Merrill Moore alone came near to writing anything like Pure Poetry. And Moore, then a medical student and ultimately a distinguished psychiatrist, was the only scientist among us. Science is officially noncommittal as to moral issues; it stays aloof from, or rejects altogether, philosophy and religion. Possibly the poetry of Merrill Moore has more moral and intellectual or even political implication than he would have been willing to concede. He could hardly have escaped altogether the contagion of thoughtfulness that pervaded the group.

Yet in general Moore's poems tended to be mere observations of the phenomenal aspects of life, unaccompanied by judgments, and very early these took the form of libertine sonnets, written in what seemed like marvelous improvisation. Moore's fertility in the composition of such sonnets is unprecedented in the history of poetry, and I am sure will remain a unique accomplishment. If poetry is but a noncommittal observation of phenomena, there is never any point at which the poet can focus and linger. One point is as good as another, and there are an infinite number of points. Then it is not after all surprising that Merrill Moore, a poet-scientist with a very quick eye and pen, should have composed upwards of 50,000 sonnets during his lifetime — an all-time record. In 1938 he published one thousand of them in a single volume.[10]

10. *M: One Thousand Autobiographical Sonnets.* I might add that Jesse Stuart, who was a student at Vanderbilt in 1931-32, seems to be Moore's nearest competitor in sonnet-writing. Stuart's *Man with a Bull-Tongue Plow* (1934) contains 703 poems in sonnet form.

Almost any of these sonnets will be as good examples of Pure Poetry, or poetry in the abstract, as our era can offer. "The Noise That Time Makes" is a representative specimen. I quote it because it can be taken to mark the stage at which Moore, after a little temporizing in other directions, took off decisively in the pure linear progression that would make him the world's champion sonnet writer.

THE NOISE THAT TIME MAKES[11]
By Merrill Moore

The noise that Time makes in passing by
Is very slight but even you can hear it
Having not necessarily to be near it,
Needing only the slightest will to try!

Hold the receiver of a telephone
To your ear when no one is talking on the line
And what may at first souнd to you like the whine.
Of wind over distant wires is Time's own
Garments brushing against a windy cloud.

That same noise again but not so well
Can be heard by taking a large cockle shell
From the sand and holding it against your head;

Then you can hear Time's footsteps as they pass
Over the earth brushing the eternal grass.

But for the other Fugitives no such course as Moore's was possible. "The form requires the myth," Allen Tate wrote in his Horatian Epode, casually enough it seemed, perhaps with an ironic bow to the classic tradition. That was in 1922. Two years later, in the April, 1924, issue of *The Fugitive,* Tate was defending the studied "casualness" of the poetry that he favored — a poetry represented, he said, by Baudelaire and Hart Crane — and was attributing its irregular use of traditional forms to lack of belief in a

---

11. *The Fugitive,* Vol. IV, No. 4 (December, 1925).

dominant "myth." "Poetry, the oracle, is gone," he wrote. "Our time cleaves to no racial myth, its myth is the apotheosis of machinery."

Yet the practice of Tate and of other Fugitives except Moore reveals them as struggling to unite the form of their poetry with the myth that ought to belong to it: or, to use the sublime term, the religious concepts and symbols that alone can validate the merely literary concepts and symbols and establish them as poetry in a realm impregnable to the attack of skeptical science. In Ransom the line of endeavor is often toward a frank reanimation of Christian concepts and symbols, armored in the seemingly deprecatory irony used with marvelous success in "Necrological," "Armageddon," or "Somewhere Is Such a Kingdom." Others, venturing eclectically, appropriate a myth with just the casualness recommended by Tate and treat it in a similarly detached, ironic tone. Or else the endeavor is to take a thoroughly contemporary, even a commonplace, subject and sublimate it by giving it a mythologizing or quasi-mythological treatment. I found that if I used an old-fashioned dragon, in some perfectly direct, romantic way, as an image of great danger and evil, the poem did not "come off." But if, using entirely contemporary language, I could think of a flapper of the nineteen-twenties as a reincarnation of a temple dancing girl of some remote century, the result might be such a poem as "Corymba." I do not think well of that poem now, but it was the first poem of mine, I believe, that won warm praise from Allen Tate. It conformed, I suppose, to the principle that he set forth in his April, 1924, Fugitive article as to Baudelaire's theory of correspondences: "that an idea out of one class of experience may be dressed up in the vocabulary of another."

Other sorts of Fugitive poetry — paralleling but not imitating Eliot's *Wasteland* — inversely establish the primacy of myth through bitter and gloomy poems in which the absence of religious belief is directly or indirectly deplored, as an element in a tragic situation. Correlatively, too, the easy consolations of science are scorned, and the inscrutability of nature and of man's life in nature is affirmed. An early sonnet of Warren's will illustrate:

DAY: LAZARUS[12]
By Robert Penn Warren

Ever in the hot street one walks unseen
Beside you as your heels clack on their way,
Striding beside you, oracular and lean,
Who has spoken not, but who will speak some day:
"When the adder lurks beneath the shriveling fern
And the obscene wheat rots in the bearded head,
Then, in such month alone, I shall return,
Bringing remembrance to you from the dead."

And then within the flesh will creep the bone
Mortally cold, while you will wait forever
In a shattered street for the viper, the bearded grain,
Lost in a chasmed land of steel and stone
To wander at noon in a chill daylight and never,
Like Lazarus, be warmed in the sun again.

But all the while, whatever the temporary concern of the poet, the main direction of the poetry follows the principle so casually uttered by Tate: that "the form requires the myth." Or, in other terms, that the images and symbols, in fact the total economy of the poem, require the support of a tradition based upon a generally diffused belief. A skeptical poetry was a contradiction in terms — an impossibility, at best artificiality rather than art. And since a tradition could not flourish without a society to support it, the natural step was to remember that after all we were Southerners and that the South still possessed at least the

12. *The Fugitive,* Vol. IV, No. 3 (September, 1925).

remnants, maybe more than the remnants, of a traditional, believing society.

The period of experimentation ended as we drew nearer to this conviction. The Dayton "anti-evolution" trial of 1925, with its jeering accompaniment of large-scale mockery directed against Tennessee and the South, broke in upon our literary concerns like a midnight alarm. It was not the sole cause of change, but from about that time Ransom, Tate, Warren, and I began to remember and haul up for consideration the assumptions that, as members of the Fugitive group, we had not much bothered to examine. They were, as it turned out, of the greatest relevance to poetry itself, but discussion of them in the closed and intimate circle of the Fugitive group was hardly appropriate. From that moment publication of *The Fugitive* ceased to be attractive, and in fact became a burden we did not wish to carry. The defense of poetry and with it the "New Criticism" were in the making. The defense of the South, for which we were to seek new friends and allies, lay only a few years ahead.

LECTURE

TWO

Counterattack, 1930-1940
The South Against Leviathan

THESE ARE LITERARY LECTURES, AND I AM RESISTING THE temptation to comment on current Southern affairs, great though the temptation may be, and heavy, in truth, the impact of events upon Southern life and thought, and therefore inevitably upon literature and the arts in general. Nor do I propose to comment upon Southern affairs of the fairly recent past except by way of necessary orientation and reminder. But at this point I must remind myself — though perhaps I do not need to remind you — that for some decades prior to World War I there was peace between the North and South — a gentle, almost heavenly time of peace, it seems in retrospect, when old wounds and animosities were left to heal, when the North generously neglected to interfere with Southern institutions, and we were allowed without much restraint to follow our poverty-stricken, unprogressive, and on the whole very happy Southern path. The North, it is true, watched for a moment with bated breath in 1898 to see whether the South would actually be loyal in a time of foreign war. But Confederate General Joe Wheeler offered his services, and

31

Southern boys put on Federal blue to fight in Cuba and the Philippines.

Reunion had been accomplished, and for the time being nothing more was asked. The South was carrying out its part of the "gentlemen's agreement" of 1876. If I interpret the historians correctly, that gentlemen's agreement was about like this: The North said, in effect: "We are tired of fighting, and after all, you have a point, as numberless Union veterans, returning from the Southern front, have assured us *ad infinitum et ad nauseam.* You let us have Rutherford Hayes for President, don't raise too much Cain about tariffs, don't bother us in our money-making and industry-building — and we won't bother you. We'll just let you go your own way — especially in that touchy matter of the race problem." And the South said, in effect: "Very well, gentlemen, we'll sidetrack Sam Tilden, and you can have Hayes for President for whatever he is worth. We won't bother you if you won't bother us — on just one condition: slip us some of that Wall Street money to get cotton mills and things like that started. You better add some money for education, too, to make the deal look good to the folks back home. They honestly do like schools and colleges better even than cotton mills."

So we had peace, on those terms. But we are assured by a Northern historian, Prof. Paul H. Buck, in his book, *The Road to Reunion,* that the gentlemen's agreement would not have stuck as firmly as it did if certain Southern writers, by a subtle kind of literary magic, had not hypnotized the North into accepting a new image of the Southern scene. It was Joel Chandler Harris' "Uncle Remus," Thomas Nelson Page's "Marse Chan," George W. Cable's "Old Creole Days" that drew the heat and venom out of the erstwhile Abolitionists and so removed the pressure they had formerly exerted on Northern politicians.

And there was also Henry W. Grady of Georgia. The

historians have given no very acceptable name to the period I am describing. It could perhaps be called *Pax Teddy Rooseveltiana* but probably "The Peace of Henry Grady" would do even better. I can truly report to you that I am a living symbol of Southern faith in that name. When I was born, it was my mother, under my grandmother's influence I am sure, who gave me a Scottish first name — out of Jane Porter's *Scottish Chiefs,* no doubt. It was my father, a nopeful young schoolteacher, who chose for his son's middle name the name of the admirable Peacemaker — Grady. And I dutifully exulted in it until, through some uneasiness that I cannot explain, I discarded it in early college days and have since avoided it except for purposes of legal identification.

But I can bear witness from many incidents that the Peace of Henry Grady was indeed efficacious up to a certain point — and from one dramatic incident in particular. One summer evening in 1917 when I was among the trainees at the First Officers Training Camp at Fort Oglethorpe, Georgia, the fifteen training companies were marched into a grove to hear a guest speaker. He was Federal General John T. Wilder, who had commanded a unit of mounted infantry in Rosecrans' Army of the Tennessee and had waged deadly war against our Confederate forebears, under Braxton Bragg, on the very field of Chickamauga where we were then encamped. With great pride the old General told of his part in that other war. He dwelt long and, it seemed to me, with vicious exultation upon the fact that his mounted infantry were armed with Sharp's repeating rifles, and therefore did bloody execution upon the Johnny Rebs opposite him, who had only single-shooters. It did not seem to matter to General Wilder that the young men before him were descendants of the Confederate soldiers whom he had so gleefully slaughtered in 1863 with his Sharp's repeating rifles. Quite the other way, in fact. Rising to a fine oratorical climax, he made his patriotic point, which was that even as he, General Wilder, had killed Johnny Rebs in great number in 1863, so should we in 1917 proceed to kill Germans in equally great number.

It was, you might say, a peculiarly awkward moment in American military history. Frigid silence prevailed when the General took his seat after this grand peroration, but we were of course under military discipline. In fact, we had joined the Federal army. The Blue and the Gray had merged in undistinguished khaki, and we were going to cross the Atlantic Ocean in the First World War of our century to fight an alleged enemy for reasons that we had to take on faith and actually did not in the least understand. As young Southerners from South Carolina, Georgia, Tennessee we were inwardly disturbed at the crude equation set up by the old Union General. How could Lee, Stonewall Jackson, Jefferson Davis, or even Braxton Bragg be equated, as enemies to be slaughtered, with Kaiser Wilhelm, Hindenberg, and *Les Boches?* We were too inexperienced to disentangle the hard logic of actual circumstances from the earnest rhetoric of General Wilder's appeal. We could hardly anticipate that the identical social and historical forces that in 1917 could send us to foreign battle could also operate in civil life in the United States and actually demand that the South put General Wilder's equation into effect—in politics, in economics, in art, in literature, in religion. The Peace of Henry Grady veiled that ominous prospect from our innocent eyes. But the ink was hardly dry on the Treaty of Versailles, and the A.E.F. was not yet all back home when the Peace of Henry Grady was broken, without notice, and the "Gentlemen's Agreement" of 1876 abruptly ceased to operate.

I do not think it would be an anachronism to say that a "cold Civil War" began from about that moment. The

South became a major target area in a long sustained bombardment which was by no means merely verbal. Not until much later did we learn the special new meaning of such terms as pressure group, propaganda, Fifth Column, Trojan Horse tactics, infiltration, and brainwashing. Looking back, we can see that all those devices were in use during the nineteen-twenties, though the terminology of the period did not include them. Except for the vituperative blasts of Mencken and his followers, Northern criticism of the South was couched in the dainty and still fairly plausible language of nineteenth century liberalism, slightly amended by Woodrow Wilson, and with some additions, finally, from the turgid vocabulary of Herbert Hoover and the somewhat more glozing pronouncements of Walter Lippmann and other journalistic pundits of the *New Republic,* the *Nation,* and the New School of Social Research.

Much of the criticism, you may recall, was directed at the thinness and sentimentality of Southern literature—or the plain lack of literature, or art, or even literacy. We lived too much in the past, it was said. We favored a moonlight-and-magnolia type of poetry and fiction. Politically, we were Bourbons, and the Solid South was too solid. Gradually the criticism became a little more bitingly specific. We were religious bigots. We were Ku Kluxers. We were lynchers. We had hookworm, we had pellagra, we had sharecroppers, we had poll taxes, we had poor whites, we had fundamentalists. We did not have enough schools, colleges, Ph.D.'s, Deans of Education, paved roads, symphony orchestras, public libraries, skyscrapers—and not near enough cotton mills, steel mills, labor unions, modern plumbing. But we had too many U.D.C.'s, D.A.R.'s, W.C.T.U.'s, too many Methodists and Baptists, too many one-horse farms, too many illiterates, too many Old Colonels. Our women were too hoity-toity about ancestors. Our men all chawed tobacco or drank mint juleps and sometimes did both. Our preachers encouraged their flocks to indulge in religious orgies. That was, it was claimed, the only relief we could get from our dull rural life—except the lynching of Negroes. We were a bad lot, a disgrace to the United States—and the only possible salvation for us was through instruction from Northern sources.

Attacks of this defamatory sort were nothing new in Southern experience. Before the Civil War a similarly distorted and vicious picture of the South was circulated in millions of antislavery pamphlets which, in the words of a prominent historian, "stigmatized the South as a black brothel" and depicted the Southern slaveholders as brutish tyrants who forced their Negro slaves to live in filthy pole pens rather than build them houses, "beat them unmercifully with leather thongs filled with spikes, dragged cats over their bodies and faces, trailed them with bloodhounds which rent and chewed them—then sprinkled their wounds with salt and red pepper" and tore infants from their mothers' breasts to sell them to Simon Legrees.[1] Such libels became the regular stock-in-trade of the Northern politician and the crusading Northern clergyman, before and after the War.

Anti-Southern attacks of the nineteen-twenties, however, differed from earlier attacks in several important respects. Behind the vituperative particulars, so irritating to the South, we can now detect a more general pattern of condemnation in which the South was but an incidental, if important, object of criticism. It was not only Southern politics that was being held up to ridicule; it was the American political and governmental system in general. Not only religious bigotry in the South, but religion and religious institutions as such. Not only the meagreness of Southern educational provisions, but the ideal of liberal

1. Frank Lawrence Owsley, "The Irrepressible Conflict," in *I'll Take My Stand*, p. 80.

education itself. Not only the shallowness of Southern achievement in literature and the arts, but the validity of the entire Western tradition of literature and the arts, from Homer on down. Not only the disordered condition of agriculture and industry, then admittedly unpromising in the South, but the basic American principle of free enterprise in labor, agriculture, and industry.

Any close scrutiny of the polemical writing of the nineteen-twenties will, I am sure, reveal these as the larger targets underlying the apparent attack on a supposedly backward and reactionary South. Such scrutiny will also reveal the implied positive underlying the negative—that is, advocacy of a collectivist type of government, thoroughly materialist and anti-religious in philosophy, controlling education and the arts no less than the means of production, and founded upon a dialectic that would insist on a complete break with the historic continuity of Western civilization. But the argument for the collectivist system put on the disguise of liberalism and, as I have said, continued to use much of the terminology of nineteenth-century liberalism.

Thus liberalism became the Trojan Horse of a creeping collectivist revolution during the nineteen-twenties. It is not therefore surprising, in retrospect, to find that the Southern defense against Northern criticism was weak and trifling during the nineteen-twenties, where any defense at all was made. But at the time it was thoroughly surprising to some of us in the Fugitive group of poets. We had been devoting ourselves almost entirely to poetry and criticism without giving much attention to public affairs. We rubbed our eyes and looked around in astonishment and apprehension. Was it possible that nobody in the South knew how to reply to a vulgar rhetorician like H. L. Mencken? Still worse, could it be true that Southern journalists, Southern college presidents, Southern clergymen,

Southern political leaders not only did not know how to answer these and other criticisms, but actually accepted them at face value?

It was true. No real defense was being made. A kind of wholesale surrender was in progress at the upper levels of Southern society. The Trojan Horse of liberalism had disgorged a horde of social scientists. These, well provided with grants from various Northern foundations, were infiltrating the South from the top, by way of college campuses, church organizations, educational associations, philanthropic foundations, professional societies. They were well assisted by a Fifth Column of Southern journalists. Of these Gerald Johnson, then of the Greensboro (N.C.) *News,* was a typically loud and persistent voice. Despite the aspersions freely and openly cast at Chambers of Commerce by this Southern group, our business men and industrialists, out of sheer opportunism if for no other reason, tended to accept their diagnosis of what was wrong with the South.

From a business standpoint, in fact, the diagnosis offered an inviting prospect. Following the doctrines of Positivism, social science in general held that environmental factors are the chief determinant in establishing, for good or ill, the character of a society, and among these environmental factors the economic factor was primary. If, therefore, the per capita income of Southern farmers fell below the national average, it would be impossible for the rural South to enjoy as good a life as other sections. It was as simple as that. The way to make a good society out of our backward Southern society was to increase per capita income at a progressive rate. And the only way to increase per capita income was to industrialize the South. They added, as a matter of course, that compulsory education, preferably at state-managed schools, would have to be instituted, in order to condition the population to appreciate and use properly the benefits of an industrial era. This was language that business men of the South, already permeated by the New South doctrines of Henry Grady and Walter H. Page, could readily understand. Their cooperation, accordingly, or at least their indifference, was assured as to the broad program. Once the business men received from social science this particular kind of secular sanctification, their indoctrination was easy—except in the field of labor relations—and the way was open for the conquest of the politicians and most of the clergy.

Here I may seem to oversimplify a large and complex process, and indeed I do omit many marginal features of this determinism which was offered to the South as liberalism and progress. That my statement of the central principle is not too simple will perhaps appear from one or two examples. I recall asking a prominent Southern sociologist this question: Would a country housewife necessarily become a better woman if she exchanged her old-fashioned icebox for an electric refrigerator? Yes, he replied without hesitation, she would be a better woman, just for that reason.

But let me take a more notable illustration. When Chancellor James H. Kirkland of Vanderbilt was queried as to his views on the issues of the famous Scopes trial at Dayton, Tennessee, in 1925, he gave out a somewhat ambiguous statement. Vanderbilt's answer to the Scopes case, he said, is to build more laboratories. I do not cite this statement in derogation of the good Chancellor. Nevertheless it reveals how the opportunism of the period obscured the real issues.

The Dayton trial was not actually a contest between religious bigotry and enlightened science, although the small army of newspaper correspondents who attended the trial went to great lengths to represent it as such to the world at large. On one side, it is true, were certain sincere public champions of religion who no longer commanded the searching dialectic that was actually at their disposal, and so had only the most naive means of presenting their intuition of religious truth; but on the other side, even more naive, were the vain-minded modernists, all resolved to define God as science and to give the theory of evolution the status of quasi-religious dogma. But the cardinal issue was the right of the state, through its legislature, to control and administer instruction in its public schools. This right was challenged, in the evolution case, as an infringement on what is now known as "academic freedom." But it was soon evident that the challengers were actually more anxious to capture this right than to deny it, if only they could use it in behalf of their own special interest, acting through a front of progressive educationalists. In the nineteen-twenties a Southern college president would hardly have deemed it politic to explore such grave issues if he hoped to increase the college endowment by donations from the Rockefeller Foundation or the General Education Board.

The Dayton trial occurred in 1925. Five years later, in the autumn of 1930, twelve Southerners published a symposium entitled *I'll Take My Stand: The South and the Agrarian Tradition*. Between these two events there was something more, perhaps, than a merely symbolical connection. I can hardly speak for others, but for John Ransom and myself, surely, the Dayton episode dramatized, more ominously than any other event easily could, how difficult it was to be a Southerner in the twentieth century, and how much more difficult to be a Southerner and also a writer. It was horrifying to see the cause of liberal education argued in a Tennessee court by a famous agnostic lawyer from Illinois named Clarence Darrow. It was still more horrifying—and frightening—to realize that the South was being exposed to large-scale public detraction and did not know or much care how to answer.

John Ransom astonished his campus friends at Vanderbilt by openly challenging the modernist position and defending Fundamentalism in religion. I recall a tense scene on the third floor of Calhoun Hall at Vanderbilt during which Ransom, more excited than I had ever seen him, opposed Dr. Edwin Mims in vigorous argument over the issues raised at Dayton. Out of the bold and somewhat grim conviction of such moments, I should guess, grew the exacting study and thought that went into the composition of Ransom's great book about science and religion, *God Without Thunder: An Unorthodox Defense of Orthodoxy.* This was published in 1930, shortly before the appearance of *I'll Take My Stand.*

As for myself, in 1924 I had become literary editor—which is to say, principal book reviewer—for the Nashville *Tennessean.* The Dayton episode vastly fortified a resolution that had already occurred to me as an inviting possibility—namely, to lose no opportunity to advance the cause of the South whenever book reviewing or literary discussion could, with honesty, serve that purpose; or at any rate to be perfectly independent in criticism and at all times to be on guard against weakness and surrender on the Southern front, or against wrongful attack from the Northern front. It was not long, too, before I suddenly found myself writing a kind of poetry I had not practiced in the closed circle of the Fugitive group. The first of these poems was "Fire on Belmont Street." I was possessed by the vision of some plump burgher of Nashville—some devout Rotarian or Kiwanian perhaps—clumsily running at the cry of "Fire," thinking only of his own house, as yet unaware that every roof was in danger. I had a question to ask him—and myself:

But who will stand tonight
Holding this other door against the press
Of fiery muscles? Who can conquer wheels

Gigantically rolling with hot breath of iron
Against frail human fingers? Who can quench
The whitehot fury of the tameless atoms
Bursting the secret jungle of their cells?
Oh, who can stay or ever chain the dull
Gnaw of the fiery smoke, eternally settling
Into the beating heart? — There is no fire.
Only, perhaps, the breath of a Southern wind
That I have known too well in many a summer,
Drying the pulse, stopping the weary pulse,
Blowing the faint blood back in the curdled veins
Till there is no way to think of what might be
Better or worse. Yet maybe it were better,
Climbing the tallest hill, to cry at night:
"Citizens, awake! Fire is upon you, Fire
That will not rest, invisible Fire that feeds
On your smooth brains, your beds, your homes, your steeples,
Fire like a dream of Hell in all your world.
Rush out into the night, take nothing with you,
Only your naked selves, your naked hearts.
Fly from the wrath of Fire to the hills
Where water is and the slow peace of time."

"Fire on Belmont Street" was first published in 1926, in the *Yearbook* of the Poetry Society of South Carolina as their "Southern Prize Poem." This and a later award by the Georgia Poetry Society are the only prizes I ever won for poetry. A sense of crisis weighed strong upon me, and almost immediately after "Fire on Belmont Street" I began to write the series of long poems published in 1927 as *The Tall Men,* a book intended to be a dramatic visualization of a modern Southerner, trapped in a distasteful urban environment, subjecting the phenomena of the disordered present to a comparison with the heroic past.

That I was not alone in this sense of crisis is evident. In December, 1925, we discontinued publication of *The Fugitive.* A small magazine of poetry, published from four to six times a year, was too slight a craft for the voyaging some of us wanted to undertake. Meetings of the Fugitive group continued sporadically, and in 1928 we published an anthology containing selections from the poetry of eleven members of the group. But by that time the Fugitive experiment was over as an organized undertaking, and for John Ransom, Allen Tate, Robert Penn Warren, and myself a very different kind of undertaking was already in not very distant prospect. We were about to try to answer in varying terms some of the questions to which we had already been giving symbolic form in poetry. In Allen Tate's "Ode to the Confederate Dead," written in these years, is such a question. The man who stands by the Confederate cemetery in that poem, meditating "rumors of mortality" and rejecting his romantic inclination to identify the rustling autumn leaves with a charge of the "inscrutable infantry" rising out of the earth — that man is not necessarily Mr. Tate himself. He might be, in fact, some intellectualized counterpart of the plump Rotarian of "Fire on Belmont Street." The two would be alike, at any rate, in their inability to recover the past for use in the "fragmentary cosmos" of the present. On this point Mr. Tate later wrote:

To those who may identify the man at the gate with the author of the poem I could say: He differs from the author in not accepting a "practical solution," for the author's dilemma is not quite so exclusive as that of the meditating man.[2]

And Mr. Tate accepts Hart Crane's definition of the theme of the poem: "the theme of chivalry, a tradition of excess (not literally excess, rather active faith) which cannot be perpetuated in the fragmentary cosmos of today." This dilemma leads to the dramatic question:

> What shall we say who have knowledge
> Carried to the heart? Shall we take the act
> To the grave? Shall we, more hopeful, set up the grave
> In the house? The ravenous grave?

2. "Narcissus As Narcissus," in *Reason in Madness*, p. 142.

I find the same theme, if not exactly the same question, in one of Robert Penn Warren's Kentucky sonnets of this period —

> Remorselessly the evening motors pass
> Bearing men home down streets where there will be
> Doorways and windows where behind the glass
> Are lights, and faces that have eyes to see,
> Seeing but nothing, ears to hear that hear
> Nothing, red lips to cry out that cry not
> But speak, speaking quickly, for the fear
> Of seeing shadows that they have forgot.[3]

What, indeed, could we say, who had "knowledge carried to the heart"? What could we say to the urbanized Southerners of Warren's poem — or of any modern city — who had eyes to see but saw nothing, and lips to cry out but would speak only for the fear "of seeing shadows that they have forgot"? The South must be defended in historical terms as it was entitled to be defended. Some true and commanding image of its past must be restored. But that alone would not be enough. The issues that still divided North and South must be examined and faced. Calumnies ought to be refuted, and errors corrected. But it was hardly worthwhile to try to deal with the merely spectacular details of the attack then being made on the South — that is, with the pure sensationalism of what was being charged as to our alleged bigotry or race prejudice or violence or slothfulness. Behind this sensationalism was a deeper hostility, a more thoroughgoing animus. What lay back of it was something broader than sectional disagreement or political and economic rivalry.

It was the total design of the attack that we had to discover, and above all the premises on which that design was based, and the end that it had in view. In the time of

---

3. *Fugitives: An Anthology of Verse*, p. 144.

our grandfathers, the South had defended slavery, and the argument presented by Harper, Dew, Fitzhugh, and Calhoun was brilliant, and, in terms of the eighteen-fifties, it was also strong and convincing. Yet it did not convince the North in the eighteen-fifties. Still more fatally, it did not convince England in the eighteen-sixties; the foreign policy of Jefferson Davis failed, and the South lost the war. Evidently the thinking of Calhoun and his contemporaries had not gone deep enough into the premises of the Great Debate. The quarrel over slavery and the western lands had somehow obscured more vital issues. The South had fought in a good cause, but the world could always be made to think it fought for the wrong reasons. We did not want to make that mistake again.

What was the South's cause in the nineteen-twenties? It was still a good cause, we thought, but how could it be stated? It was something more than the cause of the South against the North. The conflict crossed sectional lines, and was nation-wide. It was in fact world-wide. In *I'll Take My Stand,* the book of the Twelve Southerners, we chose to describe it as a conflict between Agrarianism and Industrialism. I believe we would now be justified in defining the so-called Agrarian Movement not only in terms of its first gropings and tentative beginning, but also in terms of its ultimate broader direction and general fruitfulness of application. For brevity, I might call it the cause of civilized society, as we have known it in the Western World, against the new barbarism of science and technology controlled and directed by the modern power state. In this sense, the cause of the South was and is the cause of Western civilization itself. In this sense, too, the symposium of the Twelve Southerners should be read as the counterattack of the South upon Leviathan. That counterattack necessarily had two aspects: first, recognizing the peculiar and rather isolated position of the South in the

American establishment, we had to disentangle the true
and lasting features of the Southern tradition from the
false, the impermanent, the merely pretentious, and so
restore to Southern thought an image of the South that
would be entirely relevant and valid, and defensible in
modern terms. Second, it was no less obligatory that this
image have relevance and attraction beyond the borders
of the South. For the cause was general. The South needed
the respect and understanding of all with whom we might
have common ground, wherever they might be; while that
wider audience, if it could be reached, might itself profit
from better knowledge of our real position.

In the "Statement of Principles" which serves as an Introduction to *I'll Take My Stand* that position is briefly
indicated as follows:

All the articles bear in the same sense upon the book's title-
subject: all tend to support a Southern way of life against what
may be called the American or prevailing way; and all as
much as agree that the best terms in which to represent the
distinction are contained in the phrase, Agrarian *versus* Industrial.

It was this bold antithesis — this firm declaration of complete antithesis between the Agrarian and the Industrial —
that brought down upon us the most heated criticism in
1930 and the years immediately subsequent.

At a relatively low level were the journalistic attacks
that accused us of quixotic tilting at windmills, of "turning the clock back," and the like, or that tagged us as
"Young Confederates" or "Neo-Confederates."

The Macon *Telegraph,* for example, on September 23,
1930, in a full column editorial entitled "Lee, We Are
Here," labeled us as "Neo-Confederates" and denounced
us as "a socially reactionary band [who want] horses and
buggies and music-boxes to replace automobiles and
radios." The editorial writer said:

They want huge Georgian plantation houses with well-filled slave quarters to take the place of suburbs and industrial villages. Their housewives will wrap cheesecloth around the butter and lower it into the well instead of placing it in electric refrigerators. . . . We marvel that there is such a group alive in the South today. . . . Poverty, the Neo-Confederates should know, may be genteel, but never influential.

The book had not yet appeared at this time. When three of the Agrarians replied to this editorial attack in a letter carried by the *Telegraph,* on October 7, 1930, the editor confessed that indeed he had not read the book. All that he had to go on was the brisk exchange of public letters between Stringfellow Barr of Virginia and the Agrarians that already had begun to enliven the Southern press. The editor also admitted that he did not know what to do about the "farm problem." Nobody did, he declared; but the solution would have to be economic.

A Macon columnist, writing under the name "Coleman Hill," returned to the attack in his *Telegraph* column of November 27, 1930. He considered *I'll Take My Stand* "a high spot in the year's hilarity." "The argument presented [said "Coleman Hill"] is an exposition of a nostalgic cult owning a basis no more serious than sentiment. . . . To me it seems an amusing patter-song, nothing more."

Also typical was the acid onslaught of Gerald Johnson in "No More Excuses," a full-scale article published in *Harper's Magazine* for February, 1931. This fire-eating Southern liberal found nothing good either in the traditional South or in the Agrarian proposals. He attributed the famous leisureliness of Southern life to hookworm. "Perhaps the characteristic deliberation with which the Southerner moved before industrialism began was proof of mild manners and a philosophical mind; but perhaps it was merely a symptom of uncinariasis." Johnson vowed that the South could "erect a glittering civilization in the midst of industrialism."

At a decidedly higher level were such objections as were raised by W. T. Couch, then Director of the University of North Carolina Press, who accused us of serious error in "interpreting Southern life in terms of industrialism *vs.* agrarianism." Mr. Couch was so much concerned that he devoted nearly all of his Introduction to *Culture in the South,* a 700-page symposium that he was editing and publishing, to a fervid discussion of our "error." In doing so he all but omitted to declare the actual purpose of the thirty-one articles he had brought together in his own book. We were most rash, said Mr. Couch, in assuming "that farming in the South is an attractive and healthy occupation, peculiarly devoted to the service of genuinely human purposes, and that industry is necessarily a destroyer of human values." He denied, too, that agrarianism *vs.* industrialism, taken in the Southern situation or any other situation, could be equated with an antithesis between "individualism" and "collectivism."

I cite Mr. Couch's remarks to illustrate the more earnest and thoughtful of the numerous criticisms directed at us. They also suggest just how far off one of the finest Southern minds of the period could be in failing to grasp the main point of *I'll Take My Stand* and the body of thought that went into it. Whatever criticisms Mr. Couch might offer today, they would not, I am sure, take the form he gave them in 1934.

At any rate, in the nineteen-thirties, we insisted that the opposition between agrarianism and industrialism was inherent and inescapable and defended that view not only in books, pamphlets, articles, and letters but in a series of formal public debates.

The first and probably the most notable of these debates, sponsored by the Richmond *Times-Dispatch,* took place at Richmond, Virginia, on November 14, 1930, shortly after the publication of *I'll Take My Stand.* The question was: "Shall the South Be Industrialized?" An audience estimated at 3,500 gathered to hear Stringfellow Barr, then editor of the *Virginia Quarterly Review,* speak for industrialism and John Crowe Ransom for agrarianism. Sherwood Anderson, presiding as "moderator," declared that he himself was far from neutral. He proposed to be, he said, "a worm in the apple of progress." Mr. Barr, while conceding some ornamental merit to the Southern tradition, argued that it must give way to "regulated industrialism." To remedy the evils of industrialism he proposed a New Deal program: promotion of collective bargaining through labor unions, pensions, unemployment insurance, in general the use of large powers by the central government.

In reply, John Crowe Ransom accused Mr. Barr of using the Southern tradition "as a gardenia to stick in his buttonhole when he goes traveling in New York." In general indictment, Ransom said:

> Since he wants state action, he is a laborite — he is prepared to let labor become a political party and run the government, as in Great Britain. Socialism of the variety practiced in a halfway house like Great Britain is a program of regulation which is merely temporary. It approaches every day closer to communism. The old Southern instinct which identifies the two is perfectly right in the long run. . . . Big business, which he accepts, and which every day becomes bigger business, will call for regulation, which every day will become more regulation. And the grand finale of regulation, the millenium itself of regulated industrialism, is Russian communism.[4]

4. "Whither Dixie? Mr. Barr and Mr. Ransom in the Great Debate at Richmond," by Donald Davidson (Chattanooga *News*, November 22, 1930).

Other debates were held at Chattanooga, Atlanta, New Orleans, Nashville, and Columbia (Tenn.). Members of the Agrarian group also appeared in panel discussions at various places, as at Northwestern University in April, 1937. At the Atlanta debate, held at Emory University, Mr. Ransom's opponent was William D. Anderson, Macon manufacturer (Feb. 13, 1931). On this occasion Mr. Anderson brought with him several

Ransom's indictment of Barr's position seems prophetic in the light of what the United States is becoming, or has become, in 1957. But it is not surprising, of course, that the Agrarians here and there might now like to revise the views they set forth in the nineteen-thirties.

As recently as 1952, one or two of the leading Agrarians confessed publicly that the sharp emphasis upon the opposition between Industrialism and Agrarianism was perhaps a strategic error.[5] The term *agrarian,* in particular, did not convey all that they meant, or ought to have said, in 1930. Some merit must be conceded to this view, but it is entirely *ex post facto.* It does not appear, from the historical context of the late nineteen-twenties, when we were engaged in discussion of issues and strategy, that any other terms would have served our purpose better at the time, or, for that matter, would do much better now. Industrialism represents, we agreed in 1930, "the decision of society to invest its economic resources in the applied sciences." And if it is asserted, as was being asserted in the nineteen-twenties, that the economic interest is paramount, then you are faced with the dominance of industrial economics to the exclusion of all other considerations, and after that, with the dominance of the modern Leviathan state as the manager of the total economic system. The lover of human dignity and freedom then has no choice but to oppose the resulting dictatorship and to draw unfavorable comparisons between its enforced mechanical conformity and the humane freedom of a stable, traditional society.

Such societies throughout the history of Western civili-

employees of the Bibb Manufacturing Company who, after Mr. Anderson had spoken, came before the audience and in trained seal fashion recited the great happiness and contentment they enjoyed under the beneficent management of Bibb Manufacturing Company.

5. *Shenandoah,* Washington and Lee University, Summer, 1952.

zation have generally found their economic base in the culture of the land, and may be regarded as agrarian in principle. Such was the American Republic in its original foundation, and such was the still agrarian South in the nineteen-twenties. With all its imperfections, our native South was the best available existing model of the traditional society that we proposed to set in contrast with the giant industrialism, anti-traditional in all its features, that had possessed the North and many other parts of the United States. In championing this South we were abandoning the defensive attitude of the nineteenth century South. We were rejecting the defeatism of Walter Hines Page and Henry Grady and the servile collaborationism of the modern Southern liberals. For the first time since Lee's invasion of Pennsylvania in 1863 we were taking the South into an offensive movement. We were attacking, not retreating. But this time it was to be an intellectual offensive, executed at the highest level and in the broadest terms that we could command.

On this point I would like to quote Mr. Richard M. Weaver of the University of Chicago faculty, who has found merit in this procedure. The experience of the Agrarians, he writes, "had led them to look at the South in the broad picture of Western civilization. What they saw — what they had to see — was that the South with its inherited institutions and its system of values, was a continuation of Western European culture and that the North was the deviation. That discovery takes on significance as soon as one reflects that by rule the deviation, and not the continuation, requires the defense. Thus there appeared a logical ground for putting the South in the position of plaintiff and the North in that of defendant, a reversal of the roles which had been played for a hundred years."[6]

6. *Shenandoah*, Summer, 1952, p. 4.

Mr. Weaver further notes that some of the Agrarians were poets, and were therefore committed to "the realm of value." "This meant that their judgments were to be in part ethical and aesthetic. They were thus concerned immediately with the *quality* of the South; and this orientation put the case upon an independent footing. . . . Claims based upon ethical and aesthetic considerations . . . cannot be ignored at any time, and it was these which furnished the principal means of attack."

This strategy, I can assure you, did not develop instantly. It was no hasty improvisation but grew out of years of discussion and study. Of the Twelve Southerners that joined in the Agrarian symposium, only four were practicing poets of the old Fugitive group: Ransom, Tate, Warren, and myself. In the wider sphere of interests that presently engaged us we rapidly found kindred spirits who shared our deep concern about the future of the South, in the field of affairs no less than in arts, ideas, and literature. Nearly all of these were faculty members or students at Vanderbilt, at one time or another. To call the roll of these men is to reveal the variety of interests and capacities that for some four or five years gave to the cause of the South the intense devotion that in 1930 produced the book, *I'll Take My Stand,* and, in the end, vastly more than that one book.

I call the name of Andrew Nelson Lytle of Tennessee, warm-hearted and keen of spirit, the descendant of generations of prominent Tennessee planters of the old stock. At his Murfreesboro home we often had gatherings. Educated at Vanderbilt University and in France, Lytle had also studied playwriting under Baker at Yale. But in these years, absorbed in Southern history, he was at work on his biography of General Bedford Forrest, published in 1931. In my mind I carry a picture of the Andrew Lytle of those days, eager and bold, standing on the "point" of Monteagle Mountain where Forrest himself stood in 1862 to watch, in the wide valley below, the movements of Federal columns seeking confidently — too confidently — to entrap him.

And I call the name of the late Frank Lawrence Owsley, then our young but already distinguished professor of history at Vanderbilt, a noted specialist in the foreign diplomacy of the Confederacy, yet a man of broad intellectual interests who steadfastly refused to fence himself off in one academic field. Owsley was an early and intimate friend of the Fugitive group of poets. At one time he had tried his hand at prose fiction. There was never a session of the "Agrarian" group that was not enlivened by the tale-telling of Owsley and Lytle as they swapped stories from their boundless arsenal of reminiscence. One of these stories, told by Owsley about his own "Uncle Dink," later became the basis of Lytle's remarkable novel, *The Long Night*.

I call the name now of the man you know so well — John Donald Wade of Georgia, educated at the University of Georgia, Harvard, and Columbia. One of the editors of the *Dictionary of American Biography*, John Wade had joined the Vanderbilt English Department in 1928 to take special direction of advanced research in American literature. In that field his great biography of Augustus Baldwin Longstreet was already a landmark. Our growing interest in the religious institutions of the South made John Wade a particularly welcome recruit in our historical and speculative explorations. No layman and few if any preachers knew the history of Methodism as he did — or, for that matter, the general religious life of the South. In the late nineteen-twenties Wade was writing his biography of John Wesley. It was published in 1930, the year of *I'll Take My Stand*. But most of all it was the unique personal attraction of John Wade as John Wade that drew us to him as he more and more enriched our councils with his wit and wisdom, his knowledge of men and manners, his eloquence salty and profound. There was no tale of Owsley's or Lytle's that John Wade could not match from the Georgia side. Affection grew as some of us began to visit him in his home surroundings at Marshallville, among his peach orchards, camellias, and wide plantation acres. To John Wade and to his mother, Ida Frederick Wade, my family and I owe a particularly warm debt of reverence and gratitude, for through them we first came to know this beloved fair country of Middle Georgia in the only way it can really be known — by living in it.

I call the name of Lyle H. Lanier of Nashville, Tennessee, then a young instructor in psychology at Vanderbilt, but already profoundly learned in philosophy, science, history, and the arts as few psychologists are in these times. Lanier was too brilliant a man for the North to let us keep. After holding positions at Vassar College and New York University, he became head of the department of psychology at the University of Illinois.

I call the name of Herman Clarence Nixon of Alabama, whom we had known in the early twenties as a member of the political science department at Vanderbilt University. In 1930, however, Nixon was professor of history at Tulane University. He combined a remarkable array of talents, for Nixon was then, as he still is, an economist, a political scientist, a historian, and above all a vigorous, salty, and fluent writer. Moreover, he had a knowledge of both the theory and practice of agriculture, for he owned and managed farm land near his Piedmont, Alabama, home. (At this point I might also note that Owsley, Lytle, Lanier, and Wade either owned farm property themselves or were directly involved in the management of farm land at the time when *I'll Take My Stand* was published.)

To these important figures and to the four poets of the

Fugitive group we added certain others as contributors:

— Henry Blue Kline, then a recent M.A. in English of Vanderbilt University, a young man already mature in philosophic thought. In later years Kline worked out freight differential studies for TVA, and subsequently joined the editorial staff of the St. Louis *Post-Dispatch*. At the time of his decease he was on the staff of the Atomic Energy Commission.

— The distinguished and beloved Southern writer, Stark Young of Mississippi. At this time, I believe, only Allen Tate, of our number, knew Stark Young personally, but our invitation to contribute brought us into close touch with him. I recall with much gratitude that Stark Young gave my own essay, "A Mirror for Artists," a very close critical reading before we went to press. (There were a great many such interchanges of manuscripts among us.)

— John Gould Fletcher of Arkansas, the poet whom some of us had met during the Fugitive period and with whom we had corresponded from time to time. Fletcher, in 1930, was still in England; and Robert Penn Warren was at Oxford, on a Rhodes scholarship.

These were the Twelve Southerners, the contributing authors of *I'll Take My Stand*.

But outside this circle of twelve were other figures, not contributing through written articles, to whom we owed a debt. The great Southern historian, Walter Lynnwood Fleming of Alabama, had come to Vanderbilt in the nineteen-twenties as Dean of the Graduate School. Through him some of us had direct contact with the revisionist school of Southern historians who finally did much to offset Jefferson Davis' reported saying that if the South lost the war, its history would be written by the North. But Dr. Fleming's large mind and genial personality led us beyond all merely sectional bias. To Walter L. Fleming, in love and admiration, we dedicated *I'll Take My Stand*.

To him, the inscription says, "some of the contributors owe doctrine and example, and all would offer this expression of perfect esteem." An almost similar debt of admiration and affection some of us owed to Herbert Sanborn, who had schooled us in philosophy. To my friend and master, the late George Pullen Jackson, under whom I had spent a full year in the study of Goethe, I owed a special personal debt, for in those years Dr. Jackson was beginning his study of religious folksong in the South, soon to lead, in 1933, to his first book, *White Spirituals in the Southern Uplands.* Through him I learned, for the first time, that certain old songs I remembered from my father's singing were ballads and that others were spirituals — white spirituals. I came to know the wondrous music of B. F. White's *The Sacred Harp* and William Walker's *Southern Harmony* — all that great line of sacred song that belongs natively to our people, and yet, as a tradition, reaches back into the mists of antiquity. In that great line belongs a songbook entitled *Mercer's Cluster* (Augusta, Georgia, 1817). The author of that book is Jesse Mercer, the founder of this university. And so, through Dr. Jackson's guidance I was put in a position in 1930 and later to deny the false claim, then being widely circulated, that America in general and the South in particular lacked a true folk culture and had not any vestiges of folksong except the Negro spirituals. I could and did say, in my own contribution to our symposium: "The South has been rich in the folk-arts, and is still rich in them — in ballads, country songs and dances, in hymns and spirituals, in folk tales." And we could all agree, in our "Statement of Principles," that the genuine humanism of the South was not "an abstract moral 'check' derived from the classics — it was not soft material poured in from the top. It was deeply founded in the way of life itself — in its tables, chairs, portraits, festivals, laws, marriage customs. We cannot recover our native humanism by adopting some standard of taste that is critical enough to question the contemporary arts but not critical enough to question the social and economic life that is their ground."

In 1929, Allen Tate, then in France on a Guggenheim Fellowship, wrote to me at great length about two matters. First, he proposed the founding of a Southern Academy of Arts and Letters, similar in principle to the French Academy; he enumerated its advantages and laid out an elaborate scheme of organization and operation. Second, he listed topics for the Southern symposium that we had been discussing, and suggested contributors. The founding of the Academy, Tate said, ought logically and properly to precede publication of the symposium. But, he conceded, practical considerations demanded that we not wait for the Academy. As soon as he returned to the United States, Allen Tate, by an extraordinary stroke of persuasion, extracted from Harper & Brothers of New York a signed contract for the publication of our book, not one line of which had yet been written.

To found a Southern Academy of Arts and Letters at this time or perhaps at any other time would no doubt have been an act of vast presumption. I cite the incident, nevertheless, to show that our concerns were general and that our purposes looked far beyond any mere program of economic adjustment of the factory to the farm, or the farm to the factory. We wanted to get away from mere expedients and get down — or up — to first principles. We were saying that life should determine economics, and not economics life. Our quarrel was not with industry or science in their proper role, but with industrialism as a tyrant enslaving and ruling science itself, and with it religion, the arts, education, the state, thus reducing all principles to one principle, the economic, and becoming a destroyer, ready to break the continuity of human history and threatening the very existence of human society. Therefore the articles that appear in *I'll Take My Stand* include only one article, written by H. C. Nixon, on economics in its special application to industry and farm in the South. The remainder deal with the general theory of industrialism and agrarianism, and with literature and the arts, history, education, the philosophy of progress, religion, the life of the farm, manners, tradition, the human character.

What we hoped for was that *I'll Take My Stand* would offer occasion for public discussion of these great matters at a much higher level than was then obtaining in the South or in the nation at large. There was, as it turned out, a vast amount of public discussion, but it centered far too often on mere expediency — on the economic problem of the farm or the factory, in complete isolation from the larger issues we were striving to raise. We wanted to talk in terms of the quality of life, in the South and elsewhere; but our critics insisted on quantitative judgments. To that extent they were already corrupted by industrialism. Mentally they inhabited a world simplified down to a bleak and mechanical process of production and consumption. Inevitably they mistook the immediate occasion of this book — the contemporary conflict between industrialism and agriculture — for its total purpose.

The occasion is now far behind us. The South is more heavily industrialized than ever, even on its farms, and farming as a way of life hardly survives in the South or anywhere else. To that extent the authors of *I'll Take My Stand* can be said to have lost a battle, in so far as they might be interpreted as contending in 1930 in behalf of a specific program for agriculture and industry. But they cannot be said to have lost the war, for their total purpose now shines forth more clearly than ever in the light of events, past and present. It takes on sharper relevance as each relentless moment compels the South and the nation to face the result of choices made nearly three decades ago. What that total purpose was, the critics of 1930 could have said, if they had taken the trouble to notice that Ransom's *God Without Thunder* and Wade's biography of Wesley appeared in that same year of 1930, and had striven to link them with *I'll Take My Stand,* and with the works that had preceded these notable volumes, and other works that speedily followed.

There might be many ways of saying now what the total purpose was. We might frame it in terms of Allen Tate's view, set forth in 1945, in his essay, "The New Provincialism." There he says: "Regionalism without civilization — which means, with us, regionalism without the classical-Christian culture — becomes provincialism; and world regionalism [now familiarly known as the one-world concept] becomes world provincialism. For provincialism is that state of mind in which regional men lose their origins in the past and its continuity into the present, and begin every day as if there had been no yesterday." It is, in short, life without principle, which is hardly life at all above the bestial level — that is to say, the low-grade but often pretentious life reflected in the succulent pages of *Life* and *Time,* in the T-V show, in the blaring radio with its singing commercials, and in the stream of "remorseless motors" on street and highway. To this we oppose what Mr. Tate defines as "the classical-Christian world, based upon the regional consciousness, which held that honor, truth, imagination, human dignity, and limited acquisitiveness could alone justify a social order however rich and efficient it may be; and could do much to redeem an order dilapidated and corrupt, like the South today, if a few people passionately hold those beliefs."

That would describe very well the total purpose of *I'll Take My Stand,* viewed *sub specie aeternitatis.* But also in terms of 1957 it would, I am sure, be acceptable to Richard Weaver, the author of that powerful book, *Ideas Have Consequences;* or to Russell Kirk and many other leaders in the conservative movement now strongly resurgent throughout the United States.

But I would here prefer to return to Mr. Tate's saying, "The form requires the myth," which I mentioned in last evening's lecture. In the context where it appears — one of Mr. Tate's early poems — it is a classical Greek way of declaring that poetry is impossible without religious belief. And so too is any other high endeavor, whether in behalf of the South or any other region or nation. A culture is the form society takes when it is actually "social," but it, too, "requires the myth," or else lapses into formlessness or some brutal mechanical pattern. This is the stage of cultural disintegration that Yeats had in mind when he wrote "The Second Coming" — the stage when "The best lack all conviction, and the worst are full of passionate intensity." Our total purpose was to seek the image of the South which we could cherish with high conviction and to give it, wherever we could, the finality of art in those forms, fictional, poetical, or dramatic, that have the character of myth and therefore, resting on belief, secure belief in others, and, unlike arguments, are unanswerable, are in themselves fulfilled and complete. Such was the total purpose, of which the so-called "Agrarian" movement was but a declaratory preface. From that central conviction have stemmed the poetry and essays of Ransom and Tate, the poems and novels of Robert Penn Warren, the novels of Andrew Lytle, of Caroline Gordon, and much more besides. And all these are, in their varied individual ways, the South against Leviathan, or in more positive terms, the South for the Southern tradition and our heritage of Western civilization. In the modern world there is no other way for the Southern writer to enjoy and use his rightful heritage and still be in any true sense a Southern writer. For otherwise he will — as John Ransom at Richmond charged Stringfellow Barr — merely wear his Southern tradition as a gardenia in his buttonhole for traveling in New York; or else, renouncing it entirely, lapse into servile imitation and mere topicality.

In the spring of 1933 it happened that Seward Collins, the Northern editor of *The Bookman,* wrote some of us that he wished to found a new magazine, called the *American Review,* for the special purpose of publishing the writings of four groups of traditionalists or conservatives: the Humanists of the North, the Neo-Thomists of France and America, the Distributists of England, and the Agrarians of the South. Mr. Collins came to Nashville for a conference, and there was great discussion at Nashville. Then the meeting was adjourned to the farm home of Andrew Lytle's father at Guntersville, Alabama. At that time I was on leave of absence, spending my first year in Georgia, in quarters adjacent to John Wade's home at Marshallville. I was summoned to the Guntersville conference, and took a long and devious bus journey to get there. It was a memorable gathering, as you may well guess, with ample hospitality and talk fully as ample as the hospitality. It lasted far into the night.

But it is a moment of my return trip that lingers most clearly in my mind. I had some hours to wait between buses at Rome. I walked about the city. I looked at the statue of Bedford Forrest. I looked at the bronze she-wolf suckling the infants Romulus and Remus on the lawn of the municipal building. Then I climbed a high hill, overlooking the meeting of the Coosa and Oostenaula, and found, set apart in a large and beautiful cemetery, a section devoted to the fallen warriors of the Confederacy. There I looked upon the tombs of the Confederate dead, but not at all with the eyes and mood of the desolate young

man in Mr. Tate's great poem. In the sparkling light of
that Sabbath day, after the meeting of the night before,
with hopeful prospects ahead, I was not in the least desolate. On the Confederate monument there I found an
inscription, the like of which I had never seen before nor
have seen since. I copied it. Later I gave it to Stark Young
to print in his *Southern Treasury of Life and Literature*.
It has in it, I believe, the knowledge that is "carried to the
heart":

This monument is the testimony of the present to the future
that these were they who kept the faith as it was given them
by the fathers. Be it known by this token that these men were
true to the traditions of their lineage. Bold, generous, and free,
firm in conviction of the right, ready at their country's call,
steadfast in their duty, faithful even in despair, and illustrated
in the unflinching heroism of their deaths, the freeborn courage of their lives. How well they served their faith, their people
know; a thousand battlefields attest; dungeon and hospital
bear witness. To their sons they left but honor and their
country. Let this stone forever warn those who keep these
valleys that only their sires are dead; the principles for which
they fought can never die.

LECTURE

THREE

The Southern Writer and the Modern University

MY SUBJECT CAN BE STATED IN THE FORM OF QUESTIONS
that are framed in one way if you take the point of view
of the writer, in another way if you approach the problem
as an administrator or faculty member.

Does the writer need the kind of education offered at a
modern university? One would think that he does. A growing popular assumption is that everybody does. But the
available evidence by no means supports that assumption
altogether, for the writer at least.

It is just as much in point to put the question the other
way: Does the modern university need the writer? Apparently the modern university does not think so, if we
may judge its thought from the physical provisions that it
makes on its campus for almost everybody but writers, and
from the emphasis disclosed in its curriculum and academic requirements. The modern university seems to be

Delivered before the Faculty of Mercer University on the afternoon of
November 21, 1957, as an informal "talk" from notes rather than as a
formal "lecture." As here presented, the "talk" is given in a somewhat
more finished and slightly expanded form.

saying that it needs a high proportion of Ph.D.'s, laboratory specialists, administrators, office workers. It shows an almost pathological concern for its football coaches. It employs a few librarians. But it does not want much in the way of writers. The university will tolerate a certain amount of instruction in writing if it can be scaled to fit its regularly accredited courses, and it does actually require instruction in writing for its freshmen. The university will also promote writing if it can be given a vocational turn, as in departments and schools of journalism. But for the writer in his broadly creative role — the writer as artist — the universities evidently have felt no particular need until rather recently, when writers-in-residence have been given academic status and other innovations have been introduced at a number of institutions. This is a new tendency that I shall discuss presently.

Now let me return to the first question — whether the writer as artist needs the higher education offered by a modern college or university — and look at a few notable examples, by way of surveying the scattering evidence.

William Faulkner studied only briefly at the University of Mississippi. He does not appear to have suffered from not having gone through to attain a B.A., with a major in English.

John Gould Fletcher went to Harvard, but left without taking his degree. In his autobiography, *Life Is My Song,* Fletcher records that he found practically nobody at Harvard who was interested in writing poetry — or even interested in poetry as an art. In that matter he had to instruct himself independently, first in Boston, later in France. If a John Gould Fletcher were to go to Harvard today, he would find a changed situation, for Mr. Archibald MacLeish, a poet not a scholar, occupies the chair of poetry. Would Mr. MacLeish's instruction benefit a John Gould Fletcher? An answer to this question will hinge, at least in part, on your estimate of Mr. MacLeish as teacher and as a model for poets. It is an estimate that I am not prepared to make, but I would note that the influence of Harvard as felt throughout the United States can hardly be described as "poetical" or even "literary."

And there is Thomas Wolfe, to take an entirely different case — and not a very clear one. Thomas Wolfe went to the University of North Carolina where, among other things, he studied playwriting in Frederick Koch's "Carolina Players" workshop course. Later, at Harvard he took Baker's famous "47 Workshop" course in playwriting. Then Wolfe turned out to be, not a playwright at all, but a novelist of a peculiarly torrential and formless sort. Neither from his regular academic studies nor from his extensive and special work in playwriting did Wolfe ever acquire control over the art form that he practiced. We are assured, that, but for his editor, Maxwell Perkins, Wolfe might not have achieved publication, or at least success. Would Wolfe's case have been different if he had attended some other institution than the University of North Carolina? In his autobiographical novel, *Look Homeward, Angel,* Wolfe represents Eugene Gant's family as debating whether to send him to Vanderbilt. If Eugene Gant (i.e., Tom Wolfe) had gone to Vanderbilt, he would have been a near contemporary of Tate and Warren. He could have studied under John Crowe Ransom. Would Ransom's instruction have given Wolfe the discipline that as artist he evidently needed? This, again, is the kind of question I would not care to answer. I think Thomas Wolfe's own answer would have been a scornful *No* — if I may judge from passages found here and there in his writings.

But there is Jesse Stuart, who did come to Vanderbilt in 1932, hitchhiking his way, with almost no money in his pocket. For a while he tried to live on eleven meals a week.

Jesse Stuart came to Vanderbilt because he had heard about the Fugitive poets and wanted to study under them. His previous college work hardly prepared him for the arduous graduate studies he undertook at Vanderbilt, and he did not complete his M.A. program at this time. But almost immediately after his year at Vanderbilt he began to write at high speed and to publish — for example: the poetry found in his *Man with a Bull-Tongue Plow,* which contains 703 poems, mostly sonnets; the stories later collected in *Head o' W-Hollow;* and the remarkable autobiographical work, *Beyond Dark Hills,* which in its large first draft was presented as a "term paper" in Dr. Edwin Mims' course in Victorian literature. Jesse Stuart was a member of a class that I was then beginning to teach — a senior-graduate course in the English lyric (but not in the *writing* of lyrics).

I would hesitate to draw any definite conclusions from such evidence as this about the influence of Vanderbilt University or any other educational institution on the literary performance of Jesse Stuart. Jesse Stuart was determined to be a writer. I would guess that he would have made himself into a writer regardless of the character of his college education, or even if he had had no college education. Yet undoubtedly it meant something, something vastly important to Jesse Stuart, to be at an institution where some of the teachers were also writers and where it was assumed that high literary art was attainable by a boy from Kentucky, and very much worth attaining.

I could cite various other examples — as any of us could — of contemporary writers who have succeeded very well, or well enough, with little or no college education, or perhaps in spite of it. We could also go back into the past and recall that Shakespeare was not a university man, that Poe did not stay long at the University of Virginia, and that all of Mark Twain's academic degrees were honorary — as, by the way, is also true of the poet Robert Frost in our own time. Certainly, whatever the value of college education itself for any kind of purpose, the writers of the past, whether college-educated or not, did not have courses in "creative writing" such as are now offered. They were not members of "fiction seminars" or "drama laboratories." They never attended and never dreamed of "writers' conferences" with their panel discussions, their "story clinics," their "roundtables" on symbolism, point of view, and the narrator-observer-participant. In short, much evidence could be assembled to show that a writer does not need our present kind of college education in order to become a poet, dramatist, or novelist.

On the other hand, what I have been saying about the Fugitive group of Nashville and what can be said also about the Agrarian group that succeeded them would seem to indicate that there is weighty evidence on the other side of the question. Vanderbilt University and the education it offered, inside and outside classes, cannot be excluded as an influence in the activities of these literary groups.

And now our colleges and universities more and more seem to assume that they ought to take some responsibility for fostering the literary arts in both a general and a very professional way. Creative writing courses are becoming commonplace at all levels of higher education. Our numerous writers' conferences are sponsored by institutions of higher learning. We have the new phenomenon of the "writer-in-residence" — the already famous or at least notably successful novelist or poet who is invited to dwell in the Grove of Academe, gather disciples around him for at least a semester's space, and probably even teach a course or two. Through such means, increasingly applied since the nineteen-twenties, there has been a tendency to induce or at least to simulate the kind of activity that went on at Vanderbilt in the Fugitive days. I hasten to say that I do not claim this is done in imitation of Vanderbilt. It is simply a part of a general tendency of these institutions of higher learning to shift their ground just a little, here and there. What these institutions are doing for writers of fiction or poetry is paralleled, too, by an even more intense activity in the related arts of drama and music, as the flourishing university theatres, with their workshop courses in drama and opera, bear witness throughout the United States.

The universities seem to be saying to the writers, "We want you." But they are not quite so definitely saying, "We *need* you." Perhaps they are not yet very clear in their thinking on that question.

On the other side of the matter, I believe there are good reasons why the writer, for his part, needs the university, whatever the putative or real value of the higher education to him as an artist.

The writer needs the university because of the economic and social changes brought about by the dominance of industrialism in our lives, and the profound effect which that dominance is having upon the media of publication.

The "free-lance" or independent writer of former times — say, of the time of Poe or Mark Twain — can hardly exist today, and wherever he does exist as a serious independent artist, he is an isolated, atypical phenomenon. Mr. John W. Aldridge, in his book *In Search of Heresy*, expresses a wish for this old-fashioned, independent writer to rise up and assert himself. In particular, Mr. Aldridge wants him to renounce affiliation with universities and coteries. But the wish alone, however laudable, will not revive the old-fashioned free-lance writer. Mr. Aldridge is being unrealistic.

The free-lance writer cannot function because our life is no longer as free as it was. Mark Twain, with no B.A. and hardly even a school education, could start as a humorous lecturer and newspaper writer, and then very independently go on to become the darling of the North and an honorary doctor of Oxford University. If a Mark Twain were starting out today, he would have to reverse this process. The real beginning today would have to be at the top, with a Rhodes Scholarship and an Oxonian B.A., or something of the sort, after which would come a book or two, some stories and articles in the "little" magazines and quarterlies, perhaps a Pulitzer award, certainly one or more Guggenheim fellowships, then big contracts with the "slick" periodicals and movies, and so on back down the line to newspaper syndication, paper-backs, and finally to lectures, humorous or not.

Our situation is a little comparable to the situation of Western Europe after the breakup of the Roman empire and the rise of feudalism. In the early Middle Ages an individual, whether writer or not, had little chance of life, liberty, and the pursuit of happiness if he became isolated from feudal institutions — from his overlord of high or low degree or from the protection of the Church. The artist had the choice of attaching himself to some royal or noble patron or to the clergy — in which latter case he would himself become clerical. Under this "collectivism" of the Middle Ages the individual in his secular capacity had his "place" under the code of chivalry and the complex reciprocal arrangements of duties and rights provided by the feudal institutions, which in turn were animated and in a sense governed by the Christian religion under a united Church.

But the modern collectivism planted upon us by industrialism is wholly materialistic and rapacious. It has no "place" for the serious literary artist. He must somehow make a living, but if he traffics with this modern collectivism in terms of the market that it controls, he must descend to its materialistic, skeptical, and generally vulgar level. Mass production, when carried over into journalism, book publication, theatrical entertainment of the Broadway kind, Hollywood, and T-V, requires of the artist, first of all, that he surrender his independence — which is to say his artistic integrity. The great "slick" periodicals are mostly "staff-written," or want mainly "commissioned" articles. In any case, work submitted to them must meet their formulas and if accepted will be "processed" (heavily edited) to conform to their stock patterns, which are aimed at the mass mind. The same is more or less true of the surviving monthlies that once were actually "literary." The writer may perhaps choose whether he will enslave himself to the "slicks" or the "pulps," but he cannot be independent and engage in free-lance writing unless he can first get established and so make the market come to him. Perhaps he can do that if he can start by publishing a book or two and win at least a *succès d'estime,* rather than by the old way, now difficult if not hopeless, of starting as cub reporter and working up from newspaper to magazine to book. But how can he get leisure to write books and at the same time support himself — and perhaps his growing family — in our industrialized economy?

In this situation — which I have sketched only lightly — what wonder that the writer seeks to attach himself to a university? Among our modern collectivist institutions, the university offers the least threat to the writer's artistic integrity. It also allows some opportunity for leisure and for companionship that, if not always "artistic," is at least not anti-intellectual. So the writer is glad to flee to the modern university as a refuge, even if he has to teach courses in creative writing as the price of admission. His flight is somewhat like that of the medieval individual to the protective walls of the nearest dukedom or monastery. Indeed the universities, viewed in comparison with factories, office buildings, and department stores, do seem a little like castles and abbeys. At any rate they always have libraries, and they are not yet completely re-conditioned for the mass-production of brainwashees.

On the other hand, once in residence, the writer may quickly realize that he has not escaped from regimentation. Standardization holds sway on the campus, too. That course in creative writing — noblest of arts — carries exactly the same number of credit hours, he discovers, as certain courses in "marriage counseling," "building and management of filling stations," "personality," and "client-centered psychotherapy." Examination of the catalogue reveals that philosophy, literature, history, mathematics, music, and physics have been similarly downgraded by the leveling system of "accreditation." How can he cultivate the distinctions of high art, even of honest rhetoric, in an institution that has not the courage to declare distinctions, but levels the dialogues of Plato down to an academic equality with Margaret Mead's pronouncements on the marriage customs of the Samoan islanders? He may soon wonder whether he is on the faculty only by a kind of sufferance, but he may well reflect also that the recognition of writing as a subject of at least equal importance with a sociology course is an act of conscience on the part of the university, and may be turned to good account.

But next he may discover that the students in his class, though they are a select group, brilliant and often very talented, have after all known only the featureless life of modern industrialism and do not have much to write about except their own frustration and their sense of being lost. Still worse, their language and, with it, their thought can hardly have escaped infection from what Mr. Richard Weaver, in his *Ethics of Rhetoric,* calls "the rhetoric of social science." This is a rhetoric that, in Mr. Weaver's terms, proposes to be "neutral," and hence without "inclination," but that actually uses its assumption of neu-

trality ("scientific objectivity") to disguise its equivoca-
tions and its intention to propagandize and inculcate. For
such reasons it becomes a "base" rhetoric and inflicts great
harm upon the language that has to be the medium of
literature, to say nothing of the harm it does in other ways.
The tone set by this base rhetoric is everywhere in the
educational system. It threatens to become the dominant
tone of the modern university, and is therefore the most
discouraging obstacle encountered by the writer who flees
to the university in the hope of finding there the citadel
of the "humanities" long since banished from factory,
laboratory, and all other institutions that conform to the
industrial pattern. The resident writer may then conclude
that the first and possibly most important of his tasks is to
try to restore the all but lost art of rhetoric, no matter
what happens to the art of the short story that every member of his class assumes he will impart in not more than
nine months. He may well accept Mr. Allen Tate's definition of rhetoric:

By rhetoric I mean the study and the use of the figurative
language of experience as the disciplines by which men govern
their relations with one another in the light of truth. Rhetoric
presupposes the study of two prior disciplines, grammar and
logic, neither of which is much pursued today, except by specialists.[1]

If the teaching writer adopts such a program, then his
course becomes educational in the highest sense we can
attach to the word. That, perhaps, is the best thing the
teaching writer can do for his students: *educate them.* (In
few other courses does that end seem to be held constantly
in view.) His aspiring students may or may not then turn
out to be novelists or poets. But at least they will have that

1. Quoted from the essay, "Is Literary Criticism Possible?" in *The
Forlorn Demon*, p. 100.

much education — some grasp of the true art of rhetoric and all that goes with it.

The situation as I have described it may not seem very encouraging, and yet I do not think it is as discouraging as it looks from this account. Few educational situations are ever as discouraging as they look. Young people have an astonishing capacity for somehow getting themselves educated in spite of faculties and curricula. Maybe we are far too solemn about the programs we are constantly drawing up. It is just possible that if we adhered to a well-established Southern custom of looking the other way and appearing to be negligent, we might get some excellent results, especially in writing. That is what seems to have happened at Vanderbilt University during the period that I have been referring to in these lectures. Perhaps I ought to stop theorizing and talk about something that I know about from firsthand experience. I hope you will indulge me if, in conclusion, I read some extracts from a Preface that I wrote some years ago for a small collection of verse and prose by Vanderbilt students. They wrote, edited, published, and distributed the little volume, which they somewhat pointedly called *Pursuit.*[2] You will quickly perceive that I, for my part, immediately became involved in a *Fugitive* metaphor.

In the formal garden of higher education, the Vanderbilt literary tradition appears to be a "volunteer," at least in its origins. Nobody in particular planted it. It was not very systematically cultivated by educational authority, and certainly was not much manured with money. Nevertheless it grew. It grew exceedingly, and is now so well established that literary historians must face up to the task of accounting for it. I am content to leave that task to them. . . .

I also decline to pursue the figure of speech to the last limit of its possibilities. But it does seem profitable to remember

2. *Pursuit: Anthology of Stories and Poems.* Published by the Calumet Club of Vanderbilt University. Copyright, 1951, by the Calumet Club.

that the Vanderbilt literary tradition, in comparison with what is set down in the University *Bulletin* as our regular educational program, is a very wild growth indeed. It is something native and spontaneous — an infusion from the surrounding country into our academic enclosure. The academic enclosure was intended — as all universities are — to be a center of diffusion of knowledge brought in from points far distant in time and space — from here, there, and yonder — from anywhere but the local terrain — to be handed out again, neatly processed, for the benefit of the local inhabitants. Of course that kind of knowledge has been diffused with great success over a period of seventy-five years. But the local terrain, meanwhile, was not wholly passive. The South did not sit down quietly and wait to be benefited by Vanderbilt University. It dropped seeds within the enclosure. Unbidden, they grew, while Chancellor Kirkland and the Board of Trust were busy with other matters. And presently the University, considerably to its surprise, suddenly found itself diffusing something it had never officially provided for: the fruit of a literary tradition risen out of native stock, unregistered, unscheduled, certainly unaccredited, but all the same hardy, insistently proliferous, and sometimes as prickly as black locust.

Here, by way of interpolation, I might say that the same thing coul l happen at any time at some other Southern institution, or possibly, with less likelihood, at a non-Southern institution. But during the period from 1920 to 1940, discussed in these lectures, it did not happen just this way, elsewhere in North or South.

That other institutions, now taking second thought, would like for it to happen within their academic enclosures is quite apparent from the determined effort they have been making to buy a literary tradition by spending a tremendous amount of money on writers' conferences, employment of high-salaried "writers-in-residence," and numerous special courses in "professional" and "creative" writing.

At Vanderbilt there has never been a writers' conference — not one — and never an officially designated "writer-in-residence." The Vanderbilt curriculum has never offered more than a modest provision of courses in writing.

But it is interesting to note that the Vanderbilt alumni who in past years have shared in creating the Vanderbilt literary tradition are now in constant demand throughout the United States. . . .

I will not call the roll of these names. You know them already. A number of them are mentioned in the list of books and authors attached to the official program of these lectures. But I do want to note certain very recent additions to the teacher-writers of Vanderbilt who are carrying on this tradition. These are: Elizabeth Spencer of Mississippi, who has already published three novels; Madison Jones of Tennessee, now teaching at Auburn, whose first novel, *The Innocent,* appeared in 1957; and Walter Sullivan, now with us in the English department at Vanderbilt, whose first novel, *Sojourn of a Stranger,* was also published in 1957.

In the Preface I find myself saying that if the persons named — or others, even later — were asked "What *is* the Vanderbilt literary tradition?" they would probably say, "Please don't ask, but just let me write another story."

A kind of riddle seems the best answer. If you understand why, at the time of the Tennessee "Evolution Trial," Chancellor Kirkland met the issue by declaring that Vanderbilt would build more laboratories, but John Crowe Ransom sat down and wrote a book called *God Without Thunder* and such poems as "Armageddon," "Captain Carpenter," "Antique Harvesters," and "The Two Worthies," then you will understand what the Vanderbilt literary tradition is.

From the record it is clear that the Vanderbilt writers have been persons who have chosen to confront the world by composing poems, stories, novels, plays, literary essays rather than by entering the laboratory or its academic equivalent, and resting content with its highly special and partial, though certainly often useful, procedures. To confront the world with a poem or story means that you face it, not in the dissevered pieces, the sections and dissections, which necessarily determine the consideration of science and social science, but in its complex totality. Out of that totality you make what you can, always with respect to the whole of which the poem or story is a representation.

Such confrontation also means that there must be a confronter — a person who is a total person, willing with God's help to face the world in all his human capacity, using all his knowledges, including, most especially — as may happen at the moment of composition — the knowledge he did not know he had until he started to write.

The writer must be a somebody. He cannot be the non-person, the nobody, that science in its strict impersonality must have. Realization of the world and along with it, in one indistinguishable act, realization of self — that is what it means to be a writer or any kind of true artist. To be a writer, therefore, brings one instantly to the highest level of education. It is an intense kind of living, attended by rare, almost incommunicable moments of joy which, however, are so mixed with moments of grievous toil, defeat, and pain, that relatively few will risk becoming serious devotees of the art. Nevertheless the experience is so valuable in an educational way that cultivation of the art of writing is rightly accepted as an organic part of any truly serious educational system, even though the resulting accomplishment may never emerge as authorship in the full sense.

Obviously, at Vanderbilt . . . an unusual number of persons have been willing to take the risk of confronting the world in the way I have indicated. . . . Through Vanderbilt and its literary tradition the true life of the South — which, at heart, likes for people to be somebodies rather than nobodies — has spoken, as it could not at places where the impulse toward life was obscured by the fat, borrowed transplantations and well-clipped hedgerows of orthodox education. . . .

Long may such writers and their successors, born of this true life, bloom and fruit, wherever they find harborage.